应用型高等院校经管类系列实验教材·金融

U0792101

国际结算实验

刘昊虹／著

GuoJi JieSuan ShiYan

经济科学出版社
Economic Science Press

图书在版编目（CIP）数据

国际结算实验／刘昊虹著．—北京：经济科学出版社，
2010.7（2019.1重印）
（应用型高等院校经管类系列实验教材·金融）
ISBN 978－7－5058－9698－7

Ⅰ．①国…　Ⅱ．①刘…　Ⅲ．①国际结算－高等学校－
教材　Ⅳ．①F830.73

中国版本图书馆CIP数据核字（2010）第138999号

责任编辑：白留杰　刘彦杰
责任校对：王凡娥　王苗苗
版式设计：代小卫
技术编辑：李长建

国际结算实验
刘昊虹　著
经济科学出版社出版、发行　新华书店经销
社址：北京市海淀区阜成路甲28号　邮编：100142
教材编辑中心电话：88191354　发行部电话：88191540
网址：www.esp.com.cn
电子邮件：bailiujie518@126.com
北京密兴印刷有限公司印装
787×1092　16开　9印张　210000字
2010年8月第1版　2019年1月第3次印刷
ISBN 978－7－5058－9698－7　定价：18.00元

总　序

实践教学是高等教育本质的必然要求，是践行应用性人才培养的必经之路，是地方行业性教学型本科院校办学的重要特征。近几年来，各高校经济与管理类专业实验教学已经逐步开展，把实验教学作为教学改革的抓手、知识融合的平台以及联系社会的桥梁，然而如何进一步完善实验教学体系、提高实验实践教学水平与质量已经成为各高校亟待解决的问题。应用型高等院校经管类系列实验教材以提高高等院校经济与管理类专业实验教学的建设水平为目的，以实验教材建设为突破口，探讨高等院校经济与管理类实验教材的新方向、新思路、新内容、新模式。

本系列实验教材的编写紧紧围绕“知行合一，能力为尚，积淀特色，共享协作”的地方行业性教学型经济与管理类实验教学理念，贯彻以现代教育技术为基本手段，以实验资源共享与应用为条件，强化理论教学与实践教学互动与互补，“实践与理论相结合”和在“做中学”的指导思想，强调实验教材建设与实验课程建设、实验项目建设、实验教师队伍建设以及深化实验教学改革相结合，力图通过系列教材建设规范实验教学内容和实验项目，促进实验教学质量的提高。

（一）本系列实验教材内容与教学方式符合实验教学规律和要求。具体表现在以下几个方面：

1. 实验教材以实验项目为章节，按如下体例编写：实验目的和实验要求；实验的基本原理；实验仪器、软件和材料或实验环境；实验方法和操作步骤；实验注意事项；数据处理和实验结果分析；实验报告。当然，对于不同的课程，根据其本身的学科特点，实验教材的编写体例并不完全一致。

2. 增加综合性、设计性、创新性实验项目的比例，并逐步将科研成果项目转化为教材的实验项目。

3. 与当前流行的实验平台软件或硬件及教材内容紧密结合，符合一般软件要求。

4. 充分体现以学生为主体，明确实验教学的内涵。实验教学过程体现以学生操作为主，教师辅导为辅，少量时间教师讲解，大部分时间学生操作的特点。

5. 按实验教学规律分配学时，并且有多余的实验项目供学生利用开放实验室自主学习。

6. 内容精练，主次分明，详略得当，文字通俗易懂，图表与正文密切配合。

（二）本系列实验教材遵循实验教学规律，体现时代特色，总体来说，具有以下四个特点：

1. 与现代典型案例相结合。以培养应用型人才为原则，根据实验教学大纲，注重理论联系实际，教材具有较强的实践性、新颖性、启发性和适用性，有利于培养学生的实践能力和创新能力。

2. 建设形式新颖。实验教材分为纸质实验教材和网络资源的形式；纸质教材实验报告尝试做成活页形式，或做成可撕下的带切割线形式；在纸质教材出版，配套建有供学生实验前和实验后学习使用的网络资源。

3. 实验内容创新。对于实验教材编写内容上的创新，一是凸显应用型人才培养特色实验项目，提高了综合性、设计性、创新性实验项目的比例；二是将教师的科研成果转化为本科学生实验教学项目。

4. 编写程序严格。对实验教材的申请立项的实验教材经由学院领导及专家进行立项审查；实验教材初稿经由相关同行专家给出鉴定，最终审核后，送交出版社评审出版。

本系列教材得到各方面人士的指导、支持和帮助，尤其是得到中国经济信息学会实验经济学与经济管理实验室专业委员会的专家，广东金电集团等多家业界人士，以及各高校同行老师们的支持和帮助，我们在此表示由衷的感谢。本系列实验教材尚处于探索阶段，作为一种努力和尝试，存在诸多不足之处，竭诚希望得到广大同行及相关专家的批评指正。

应用型高等院校经管类系列实验教材编委会

2009 年 12 月

前　言

国际结算研究的内容属于国际金融领域的一个分支，是一门以国际金融、国际贸易和货币银行学为基础而形成的应用性交叉学科，它主要从微观角度探讨国际间货币运动的实务问题。国际结算是一门实践性和操作性很强的课程，而且业务操作中以国际惯例为依据的特征也使本门课程具有很强的国际性。

21 世纪以来，无论是我国的对外贸易还是银行的国际结算业务都进入了快速发展阶段。从对外贸易看，2007 年中国贸易量居世界第三位，其中出口量为世界第二，进口量为世界第三，极大地推动了国际结算业务的发展。中国银行作为中国最大经营国际结算业务的银行，2007 年国际结算业务量首次突破万亿美元大关，达到 1.4 万亿美元，成为全球银行业首家年国际结算业务量超过万亿美元的商业银行。此外，在中外资银行的竞争中，作为中间业务之一的国际结算也成为银行竞争的重要领域。因此，国际结算的重要性越来越突出。

本教材在撰写中贯彻实验操作与国际惯例、中国商业银行国际结算相结合的原则，在阐述国际结算原理的同时，通过大量的图表演示和系统性的操作练习，使学生能更直观地掌握国际结算的主要业务、操作程序，并熟悉业务操作中的基本步骤和方法，增加学生对理论学习的兴趣，掌握各种业务操作的娴熟技巧，为走上工作岗位、尽快适应工作需要打下扎实的基础。

根据各自不同专业要求，带＊号部分为选学章节，包括实验一和实验七。

作为广东金融学院“金融学国家级特色专业”的指定使用教材，在本书撰写过程中，作者得到了中国银行湖南省分行国际业务部谭沁经济师和招商银行总行国际业务部赵刚经济师等来自金融部门业内专家的热心支持和有益的建议。广东金融学院金融系徐润萍主任（教授）对本书的撰写倾注了大量心血，王醒男主任（教授）作为本书的主审提出了许多严格又富有建设性的修改意见，在此一并向他们表示由衷的感谢和诚挚的敬意。

由于时间仓促和水平有限，书中难免存在疏漏和不妥之处，恳请广大读者和同行批评指正。

本书适合高等院校财经专业教学使用，也可作为银行相关业务人员的培训资料使用。

作者

前 言

[illegible]

目　录

*实验一

国际结算中的票据
（特色实验）

一、实验目的

1. 把握汇票、本票、支票有效性的审核。
2. 正确填写汇票、本票、支票。
3. 掌握汇票、本票、支票中各种票据行为的操作和处理。
4. 熟悉汇票、本票、支票的处理流程。

二、实验原理

国际结算是指以银行为中介进行国际间资金调拨，结算位于不同国家和地区之间的两个或两个以上当事人间债权债务的一种活动。国际结算业务研究的内容见图 1－1。

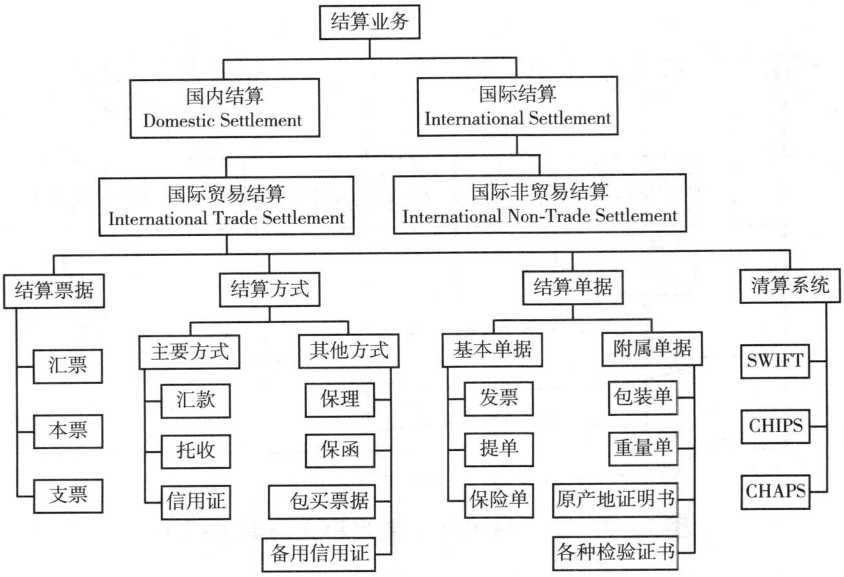

图 1－1　国际结算的内容

如图 1－1 所示，国际结算业务包括国际贸易结算和国际非贸易结算。国际贸易结算中进口商和出口商以进口地银行和出口地银行为中介，在一定的结算方式下，通过票据和单据的处理，借助银行间结算系统，进行债权、债务的结算。

（一）汇票知识点

国际贸易中，出口商开立汇票后可直接委托银行收款，进口商开立本票和支票交付出口商后再由出口商委托银行收款。三种票据的处理程序和风险点不同。国际结算中票据结算处理程序见图 1－2。

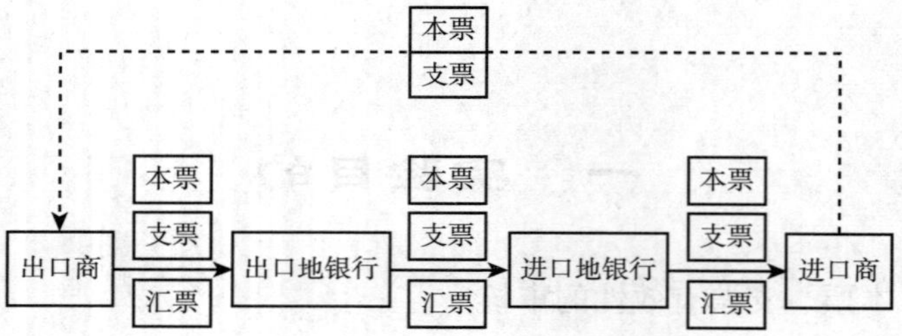

图 1－2　票据结算处理基本程序

汇票（Bill of Exchange）是国际贸易结算中最常见的票据，它由出票人向另一人签发，要求即期、定期或在可以确定的将来时间，向某人或其指定人或来人无条件地支付一定金额的书面命令。汇票从开立至最终付款，涉及出票、背书、承兑、提示、拒付、追索、保证等行为，这些行为必须在汇票正面或反面填列。本票、支票、汇票在出票、提示、背书等票据行为的处理中具有相似规定，本票、支票可参照汇票行为的相关规定处理。指示性抬头汇票当事人与票据行为见图 1－3。

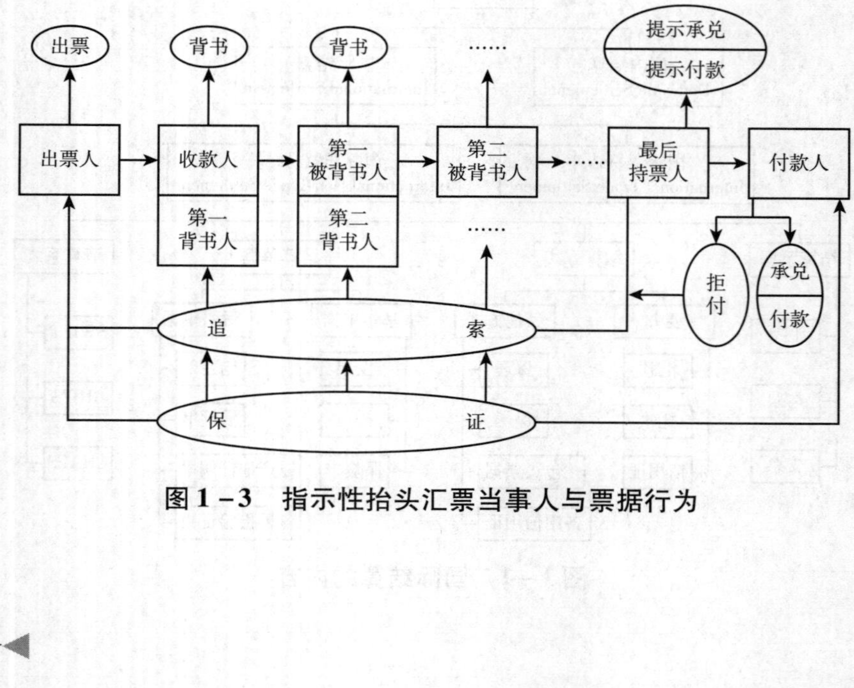

图 1－3　指示性抬头汇票当事人与票据行为

1. 汇票的票据行为

（1）出票（Issuance）。出票是指出票人签发汇票并将汇票交给收款人，它包括两个动作：一是制作汇票并在汇票上签字，二是将汇票交给付款人。汇票开立时一般包括八个必要项目。汇票填写见示样 1－1。

示样 1－1　汇票

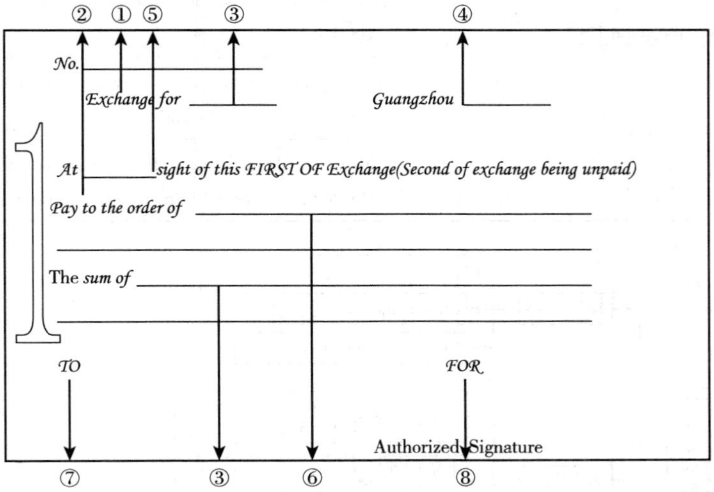

如示样 1－1 所示，汇票的八个必要项目分别是：

①汇票字样；②无条件支付命令；③一定金额货币；④出票地点和日期；⑤付款期限；⑥收款人；⑦付款人；⑧出票人。

其中，常见无条件支付命令与一定金额货币写法中有效与无效表示见表 1－1，汇票付款期限的分类与写法见图 1－4，汇票付款期限对提示行为的影响见表 1－2。

表 1－1　　无条件支付命令与一定金额货币写法中的有效与无效表示

项目	有效表示	无效表示	无效原因
无条件支付命令	① Pay to __; ② Please pay to __; ③ D/P（D/A）, Drawn against shipment of 20 bales of bombazine from Guangzhou to Hong Kong for collection; ④ Drawn under LC No. 123 issued by XX Bank, New York, dated 12, November, 2004	① I will be very pleased if you pay to __ ② I beg you to pay to __	请求
		① Pay to __ if the goods they supplied are complied with contract No. 123 ② Pay to __ providing the goods arrived at destination before 27, October ③ Pay to __ on condition that goods have been shipped on board before 18, November ④ Pay to __ out of the proceeds in our No. 456 account	有条件

续表

项目	有效表示	无效表示	无效原因
一定金额货币	USD1, 000. 00 , the sum of <u>One thousand USD</u>	① the sum of about one thousand USD	金额无法确定
		② the sum of circa one thousand USD	
		③ the sum of one thousand USD or two thousand USD	
		④ Pay to the order of __ the sum of one thousand US dollars plus interest	缺利率和计息时间
		⑤ Pay to the order of __ the sum of one thousand US dollars by installments	缺付款次数和每次付款金额
		⑥ Pay to the order of __ the sum of one thousand US dollars converted into sterling equivalent	缺汇率

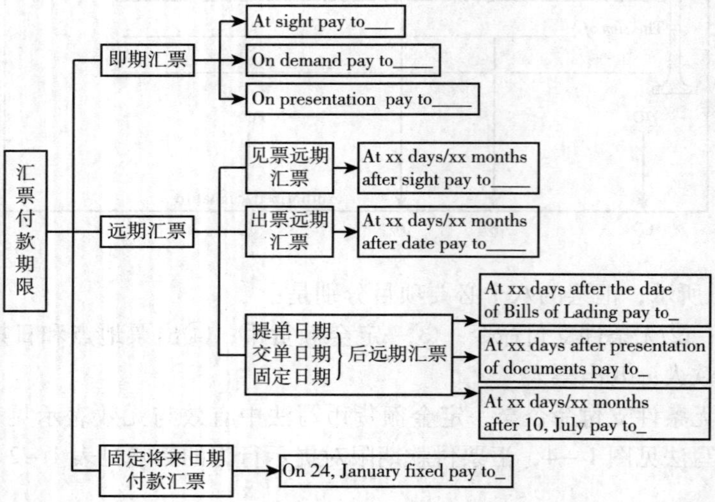

图 1－4　汇票付款期限的分类与写法

表 1－2　　　汇票付款期限对提示行为的影响

种类	提示次数	提示种类
即期汇票	一次	到期日提示付款 Present for Payment
远期汇票	二次	① 到期日前提示承兑 Present for Acceptance
		② 到期日提示付款 Present for Payment

即期汇票付款日为到期日，不涉及到期日的计算。远期汇票到期日计算中必须判断起算日并把握不同的计算方法，远期汇票到期日计算方法见图 1－5。

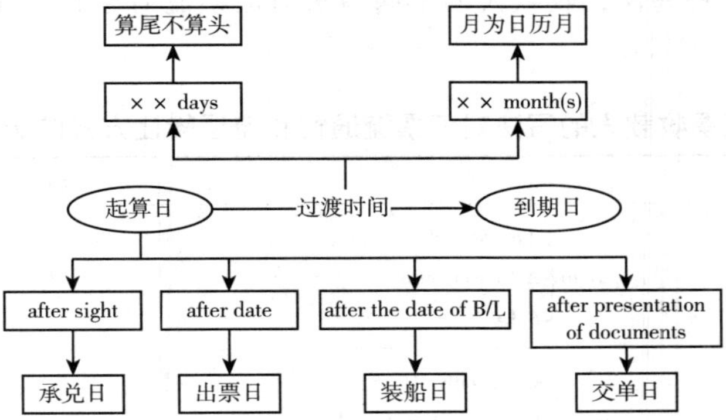

图 1－5　远期汇票到期日的计算

例一：

At 60 days after date，如汇票出票日为 7 月 10 日，则：

7 月 11～31 日……………………………21 天 } 52 天 } 60 天

8 月 1～31 日……………………………31 天

9 月 1～8 日………………………………8 天

到期日为 9 月 8 日。

例二：

At 90 days after sight，如汇票见票日（承兑日）为 4 月 5 日，则：

4 月 6～30 日……………………………25 天 } 56 天 } 60 天

5 月 1～31 日……………………………31 天

6 月 1～4 日………………………………4 天

到期日为 6 月 4 日。

例三：

At one month after sight，如汇票见票日（承兑日）为 25，February，则：

25，February ……one month……→ 25，March

到期日为 3 月 25 日。

例四：

At one and half a month after sight，如汇票见票日（承兑日）为 25，February，则：

25，February ……one month……→ 25，March ……half a month（15 天）……→ 9，April

到期日为 4 月 9 日。

根据上述方法计算出汇票到期日后，付款人一般都会在票面注明到期日，便于在到期日按时付款。

汇票收款人有三种写法，收款人的不同写法对汇票流通性和流通转让方式的影响见表1－3。

表1－3　汇票收款人的写法对汇票流通性和流通转让方式的影响

分类	写法	流通性	流通转让方式
记名抬头	pay to { the order of A Co. / A Co. or order / A Co.	有	背书交付转让
限制抬头	pay to { A Co. only / A Co. not transferable / A Co. not negotiable	无	/
空白抬头	pay to bearer	有	交付转让

实务中，常见汇票是由出口商开立的已收汇票，即收款人是出票人（出口商）的指定人，抬头人一栏表示为"Pay to the order of ourselves"。汇票抬头人为出口地银行的汇票也比较常见。

（2）背书（Endorsement）。背书是指持票人将汇票权利转让给他人或将一定的汇票权利授予他人行使的行为。背书包括两个动作：一是在汇票背面签名或记载有关事项，二是将汇票交付给被背书人或受让人。汇票背书的不同种类在写法及对汇票流通性的影响上与抬头人具有相似之处。背书的写法和性质见表1－4。

表1－4　汇票背书的写法及性质

种类	写　法	流通性
特别背书	Pay to the order of B Co. For A Co. , London signature	可再背书转让
空白背书	For A Co. , London signature	可交付转让；或以其他背书方式转让
限制性背书	Pay to A Bank { only / not negotiable; not transferable; for account of B Co. For A Co. , London Signature	不能转让
附带条件背书	Pay to A Co. on delivery of B/L No. 123 For A Co. , London Signature	可再背书转让
托收背书	Pay to A Bank for collection For A Co. , London Signature	可再背书转让

持票人应以连续不间断的背书证明其权利正当，因此银行处理汇票时应检查汇票背书是否连续、不间断。汇票背书的连续性判断见图1－6。

当事人 \ 顺序	第一	第二	第三	第四	第五	……
被背书人	Pay to B	Pay to C	Pay to D	Pay to E	Pay to F	最后被背书人是持票人
背书人	For A (Payee)	For B	For C	For D	For E	

图 1－6　汇票的连续不间断背书

托收业务中，汇票通过背书，可确保托收行、代收行作为汇票的正当持票人，有权向付款人提示汇票以获得承兑或付款。信用证业务中汇票经过背书，可使银行控制物权，降低出口押汇和议付中的风险。托收汇票背书的处理见图 1－7。

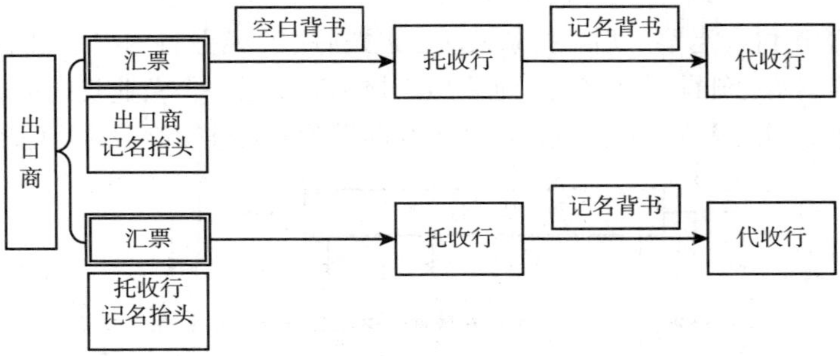

图 1－7　托收汇票的背书

（3）承兑（Acceptance）。汇票的承兑指远期汇票的付款人在汇票正面签名表示同意在汇票到期日支付汇票金额的一项承诺。即期汇票无须承兑，远期汇票则涉及承兑行为。承兑的交付方式有两种：一是实际交付，即将承兑汇票交还持票人；二是推定交付，只要付款人通知持票人已于某日作出承兑就算交付。国际上，对于 180 天以内（包含 180 天）的远期汇票，在承兑后，代收行或付款行一般都保留汇票，仅通过邮寄或电讯方式向托收行或出口地银行发出承兑通知书。承兑汇票见示样 1－2，承兑通知书见示样 1－3。

示样 1－2　承兑汇票

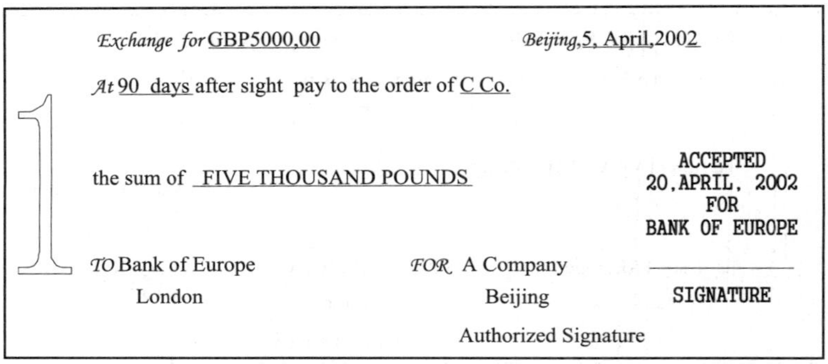
Exchange for GBP5000.00　　Beijing,5, April,2002

At 90 days after sight pay to the order of C Co.

the sum of FIVE THOUSAND POUNDS

ACCEPTED
20.APRIL, 2002
FOR
BANK OF EUROPE

TO Bank of Europe
London

FOR A Company
Beijing
Authorized Signature

SIGNATURE

示样 1－3　承兑通知书

MIDLAND BANK LIMITED

ACCEPTANCE NOTICE

London, ________________

To ________________

We give you below details of draft accepted by ourselves:

Your Ref No.	Drawer	Amount	Due	Remark

For **Midland Bank Ltd**

____

Authorized Signature (s)

（4）拒付（Dishonor）。拒付又称退票，是指当汇票的持票人依票据法的规定向付款人提示要求付款或要求承兑时，遭到拒绝付款（Dishonor for Payment）或拒绝承兑（Dishonor for Acceptance）。汇票提示遭拒付（退票）后，持票人应在退票后一个营业日内将退票事实通知全体前手，或者持票人将退票事实通知前手背书人，前手应于接到通知后一个营业日内再通知他的前手背书人，一直至最终通知到出票人。持票人向出票人和前手背书人进行追索的处理环节见图 1－8。

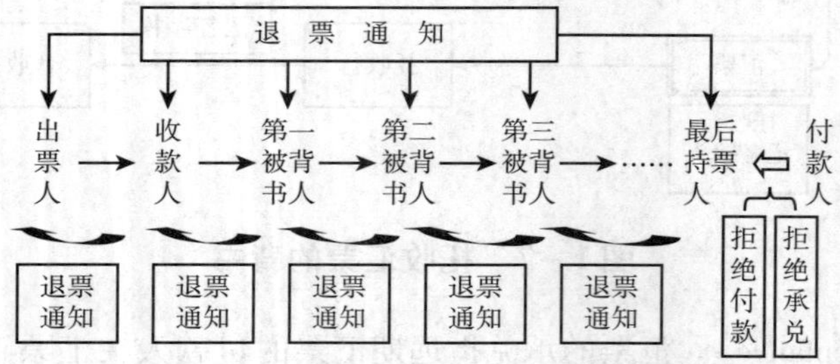

图 1－8　汇票的拒付与追索

（5）保证（Guarantee）。保证是指非票据债务人对于出票、背书、承兑、参加承兑等行为所发生的债务予以保证的附属票据行为。保证人对出票人、前手背书人等票据债务人的债务作出的保证行为在汇票正面列明。保证汇票见示样 1－4。

示样 1－4　保证汇票

Exchange for GBP5000,00　　　*Beijing* ,5, April ,2002

At 90 days after sight pay to the order of C Co.

the sum of FIVE THOUSAND POUNDS

Payment Guaranteed

Dated on 10,April, 2002

TO Bank of Europe　　*FOR* A Company

London　　Beijing

For B Co.

Signed

Authorized Signature

2. 汇票的种类

汇票的种类见图 1 – 9。

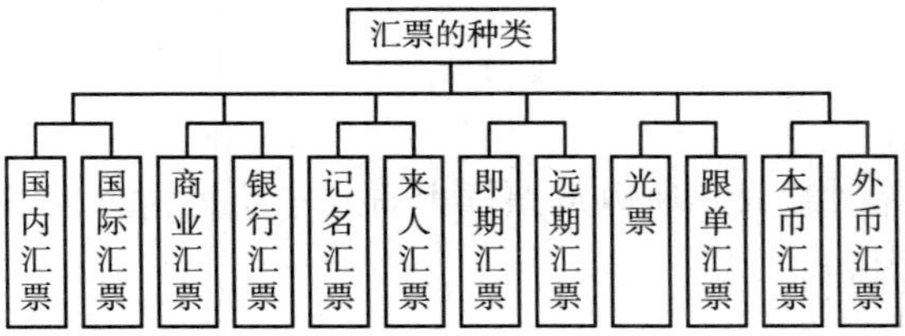

图 1 – 9　汇票的种类

如图 1 – 9 所示，国际结算中的汇票从不同角度划分可分为六大类，从不同的角度看，一张汇票可归属于不同的种类。如：一笔信用证业务中可能开立的是跟单、即期、记名抬头、以外币为支付货币的商业汇票。实务中，只有跟单汇票或个人支票可能签发远期，光票类汇票、本票、支票都只有即期没有远期，凡是较大金额的远期光票大都怀疑是假票。

（二）本票和支票知识点

1. 本票（Promissory Note）

本票是一人向另一人签发的，保证即期或定期或在可以确定的将来时间，对某人或其指定人或执票人支付一定金额的无条件书面承诺。本票开立包括八个必要项目。本票的填写见示样 1 – 5。

示样 1 – 5　本票

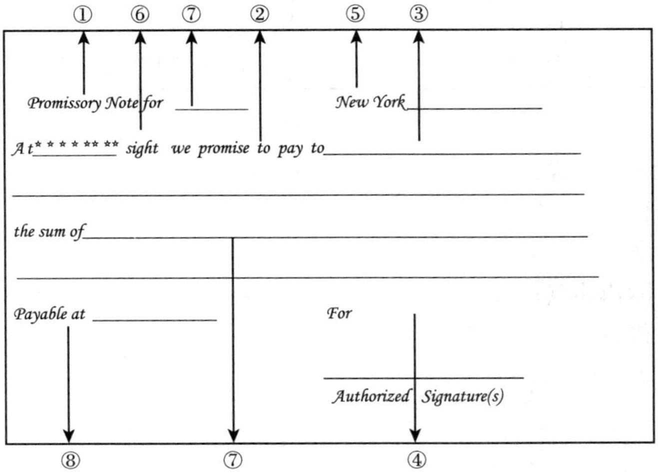

如示样 1 – 5 所示，本票的八个必要项目分别是：

①“本票”字样；

② 无条件支付承诺；

③ 收款人或其指定人；
④ 制票人签字；
⑤ 出票地点和日期；
⑥ 付款期限；
⑦ 一定金额货币；
⑧ 付款地点。

由于本票的出票人是付款人，所以从票样上看，本票无付款人的记载，同时，本票也缺少汇票处理中的承兑行为。

2. 支票（Check / Cheque）

（1）支票的必要项目和填写。支票是银行存款户对其开立账户的银行签发的，授权该银行向某人或其指定人或执票来人即期支付一定金额的无条件书面支付命令。支票开立包括八个必要项目。支票的填写见示样1－6。

示样 1－6　支票

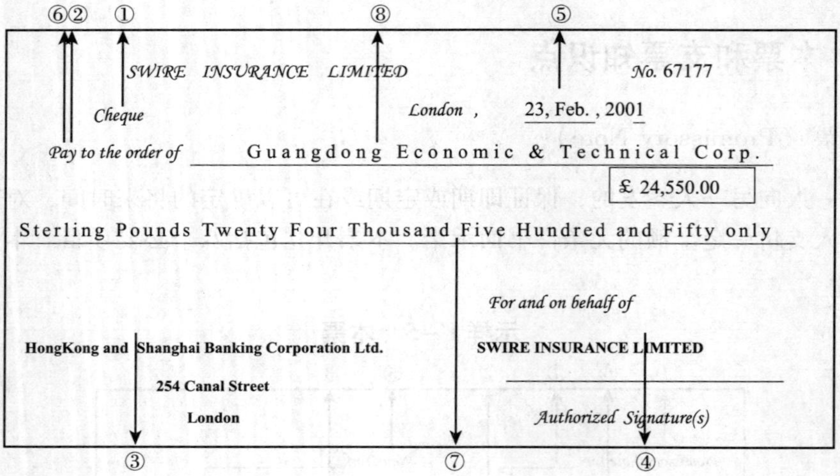

如示样 1－6 所示，支票的八个必要项目分别是：
①“支票”字样；
② 无条件支付命令；
③ 付款银行名称和地点；
④ 出票人名称和签字；
⑤ 出票日期和地点；
⑥“即期”字样；
⑦ 一定金额；
⑧ 收款人或其指定人。

支票仅为即期付款，无远期票据处理中的承兑行为。

（2）支票的种类。常见支票的种类见表 1－5。

表 1－5　　　　支票的种类、写法及特点

种类		写法	特点
记名支票		Pay to the order of sb. Pay to sb. or order Pay to sb.	可背书转让
不记名支票		Pay bearer	可交付转让
现金支票		支票上无两条平行线	可收取现金
划线支票	普通划线	支票上两条平行线内未指定收款银行	可由任何一家银行收款入账
	特别划线	支票上两条平行线内专门指定一家收款银行	只能由指定银行收款入账
保付支票		Certified Cheque	有保付行的付款承诺
银行支票		Banker's Cheque	出票人、付款人都是银行

如表 1－5 所示，支票不同的抬头影响支票的流通性和流通转让方式；支票上是否有划线决定支票的收款方式；保付支票和银行支票中有银行付款保证，收款保障性强，易于接收和转让。

（3）支票的划线。划线支票的划线一般在支票的左上角。划线支票不能直接收取现金，只能委托银行代为收款入账。普通划线支票可由任何银行收款入账，特别划线支票只能由指定银行收款入账。普通划线支票（General Crossing）见示样 1－7，特别划线支票（Special Crossing）见示样 1－8。

示样 1－7　普通划线支票

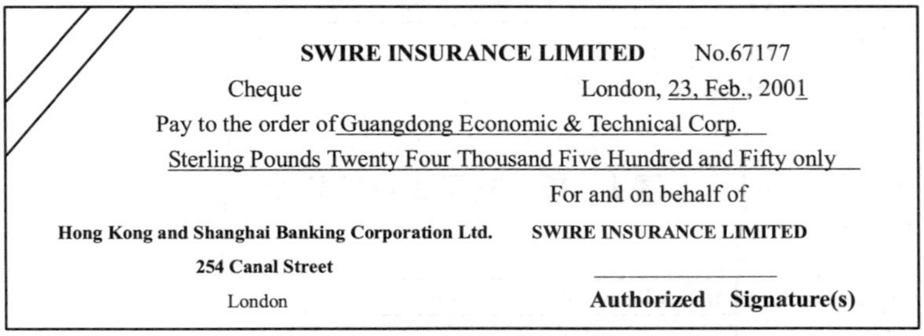
SWIRE INSURANCE LIMITED　No.67177
Cheque　London, 23, Feb., 2001
Pay to the order of Guangdong Economic & Technical Corp.
Sterling Pounds Twenty Four Thousand Five Hundred and Fifty only
For and on behalf of
Hong Kong and Shanghai Banking Corporation Ltd.　SWIRE INSURANCE LIMITED
254 Canal Street
London　Authorized Signature(s)

示样 1－8　特别划线支票

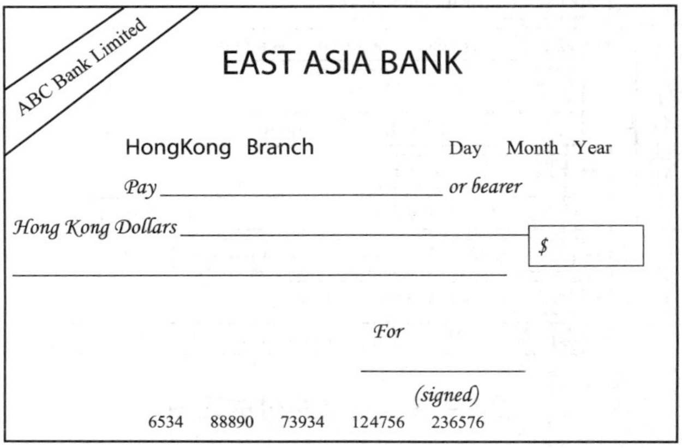
ABC Bank Limited
EAST ASIA BANK
HongKong Branch　Day Month Year
Pay ______ *or bearer*
Hong Kong Dollars ______ *$*
For
(signed)
6534　88890　73934　124756　236576

普通划线支票还有以下表示：

	Not Negotiable	Account Payee	Banker	& Co.

支票特别划线中加注的银行名称只能有一个，除非该银行又委托另一家银行代收票款，这时，一张支票上就可能出现两个特别划线。特别划线支票还有以下表示：

ICBC Bank	A/C payee， A Bank	ICBC Bank Barclay Bank for collection

出票人和持票人可以划线。出票人作成普通划线，持票人可以把它转变成特别划线。出票人作成普通划线或特别划线，持票人可加注“不可流通”字样。被特别划线的银行可以再作特别划线给另一家银行代收票款，代收票款的银行可以作成特别划线给自己。

（4）支票的止付与拒付。在支票实务中，如果支票遗失或毁坏，出于安全考虑，出票人可以止付支票。出票人若认为收款人不愿或无法执行出票人为之签发支票的合同，出票人也可以止付支票。此外，支票上的付款行也会因为支票上存在的各种问题对持票人提示的支票提出拒付。支票止付的处理见图 1－10，支票常见的拒付理由见图 1－11。

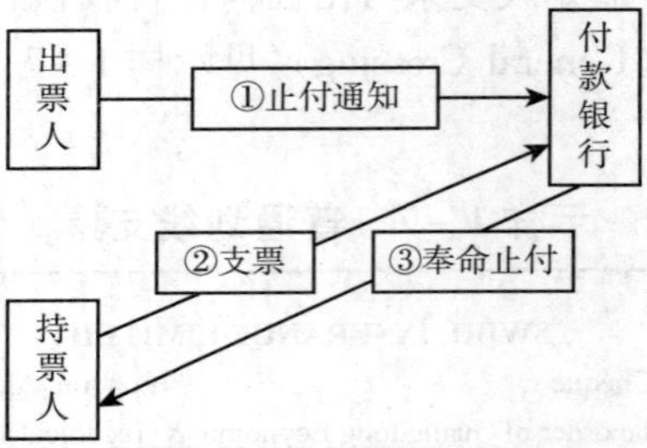

图 1－10　支票止付的处理

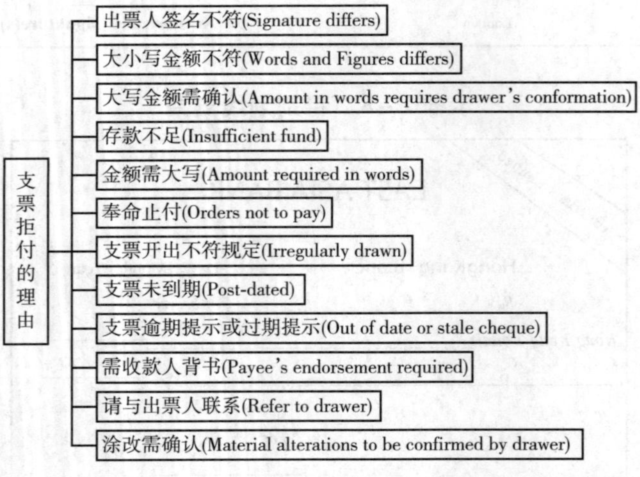

图 1－11　支票拒付的理由

三、实验内容

1. 写出并检查所给汇票的必要项目。
2. 根据所给条件开立汇票。
3. 根据所给条件在汇票上进行背书。
4. 根据所给条件在汇票上进行承兑和发出承兑通知书。
5. 写出并检查所给本票的必要项目。
6. 根据所给条件开立本票。
7. 写出并检查所给支票的必要项目。
8. 根据所给条件开立支票。
9. 根据所给条件在支票上划线。

四、实验步骤

（一） 汇票

1. 客户向银行提交汇票，按汇票必要项目和所给问题对其进行审核和处理

（1）托收中的汇票

Deliver Documents only upon ~~Acceptance~~/payment

NO.S20030117/123

New York 7, MAY, 2003

AT ********* SIGHT OF THIS FIRST BILL OF EXCHANGE (SECOND UNPAID)

PAY TO THE ORDER OF Bank of America N. T. &S. A

U.S. DOLLARS TWENTY FIVE HUNDRED THOUSAND ONLY

USD250,000	00

VALUE RECEIVED AND CHARGE TO ACCOUNT OF ____________

DRAWN UNDER SALES CONTRACT NO. 23476 AGAINST 500 BARRELS OF OIL

FROM NEW YORK TO GUANGZHOU FOR COLLECTION

TO CHINA GUANGDONG IMP. CORP
GUANGZHOU
CHINA

For and on behalf of
NOVUS INTERNATIONAL
PTE LTD, NEW YORK

Authorized Signature(s)

（2）信用证中的汇票

ACCEPTED 14th，April，2004 For Midland Bank Ltd.，London __________ Signed	Due 13th，July，2004 ①　⑤　③ Exchange for GBP56，400.00　　Guangzhou，5th，April，2004 ④　②　⑦ At 90 days after sight pay to the order of ourselves ⑤ the sum of Sterling Pounds Fifty Six Thousand Four Hundred only Drawn under Documentary Credit No. 57982 issued by Midland Bank，dated 10th，March，2004 ⑥　⑧ To Midland Bank Ltd.，　　For Guangzhou Textiles Holdings London Authorized Signature（s）

项目、问题 \ 类型	托收中的汇票	信用证中的汇票
（1）汇票字样		
（2）无条件支付命令		
（3）出票地点和日期		
（4）付款时间		
（5）付款金额		
（6）付款人名称和付款地点		
（7）收款人名称		
（8）出票人名称和签字		
（9）提示次数		
（10） ① 2003 年 5 月 7 日有什么作用（托收中的汇票）？ ②“Due 13th，July，2004”是什么时间（信用证中的汇票）？		
（11）汇票在法律上生效，以哪国法律为准？		
（12）汇票的转让和转让方式		
（13）若收款人遭到拒付，在追索时应注意哪些事项？		
（14）汇票出票后、未承兑前，Midland Bank Ltd.，London 是否为汇票的债务人（信用证中的汇票）？		
（15）收款人于汇票承兑当天请承兑行 Midland Bank Ltd 做贴现，银行按 6% p.a. 计息，计算贴现息和净款。（信用证中的汇票）		

2. 客户提交汇票委托银行收款，银行对汇票有效性进行判断并给予客户建议

汇票的无条件支付命令	有效/无效	建议
(1) Pay to A Corp. two thousand US dollars providing the goods in compliance with sales contract No. 123.		
(2) Pay to A Co. the sum of five thousand Sterling Pounds on condition that goods have been shipped on board before 23, December.		
(3) At sight pay to the order of A Co. the sum of one hundred thousand Japanese Yen drawn against shipment of 20 bales of cotton from Guangzhou to Tokyo.		
(4) At 30 days after sight pay to the order of Bank of China the sum of two hundred thousand US dollars drawn under L/C No. 1234 issued by Bank of New York dated on 20th August, 2004.		
(5) Pay to A Co. one thousand US dollars out of our No. 345 account.		
(6) Pay to A Co. three thousand US dollars plus interest at 5% from the date hereof to the date of payment.		
(7) Pay to A Co. four thousand US dollars by ten installments.		
(8) Pay to A Co. five thousand Sterling Pounds converted into US dollars equivalent.		

3. 根据所给条件填写汇票

汇票项目	汇票一	汇票二	汇票三
(1) Date and Place of Issue	10/Jan./2004, Changsha	17/Nov./2004, Tokyo	25/Feb./2003, Guangzhou
(2) Tenor	one month after date	At 90 days after sight	on demand
(3) Payee	Agricultural Bank of China, Hunan	CREDIT SUISSE, TOKYO, BRANCH	China National Animal By-products Imp. & Exp. Corp., Guangzhou
(4) Amount	GBP21, 350.00	J￥7, 082, 000.00	USD34, 486.78
(5) Drawee	AAA Group Co., Ltd., London	Bank of China, Guangdong Branch	First National Bank of Chicago
(6) Drawer	The Hunan Arts & Crafts Imp. & Exp. Company	TOYOTA TSUSHO CORPORATION	China National Animal By-products Imp. & Exp. Corp., Guangzhou Branch
(7) Drawn Clause	Drawn against 1000 boxes of glass bricks from Changsha to London	Drawn against L/C No. 235GD201 issued by Bank of China, Guangdong Branch, dated 20/Oct., 2004	Drawn against L/C No. 2431/221 issued by First National Bank of Chicago, dated 20, Dec., 2002

(1) 汇票一

Exchange for ________________ ________________, ________________ 200__

(Amount in figure) (Place and date of issue)

At ________________ sight of this First Bill of Exchange (Second unpaid)

(Tenor)

pay to ____ or order

the sum of ____

(Amount in words) ____

Drawn ____

____

To ________________ For ________________

________________ ________________

Authorized Signature (s)

(2) 汇票二

Exchange for ________________ ________________, ________________ 200

Drawn under ____

____

At ________________ sight of this First Bill of Exchange (Second unpaid)

pay to ____ or order

the sum of ____

____

To ________________ For ________________

________________ ________________

Authorized Signature (s)

(3) 汇票三

Exchange for ________________ ________________, ________________, ________________ 200__

At ________________ sight of this Second Bill of Exchange (First unpaid)

pay to ____ or order

the sum of ____

____

Drawn under ____

____

To ________________ For ________________

________________ ________________

Authorized Signature (s)

4. 远期汇票到期日的计算

GUANGDONG IMP. & EXP. CORPORATION 提交下列五张不同付款期限的已承兑汇票委托银行向承兑人提示付款。审核各张汇票后，在表格中填写汇票的付款期限并计算汇票的到期日。

（1）汇票一

Exchange for USD60 234.00　　Guangzhou, 20th, Mar., 2003

D/A At 30 days after sight of this First bill of exchange (Second unpaid)

Pay to the order of Construction Bank of China

the sum of US DOLLARS SIXTY THOUSAND TWO HUNDRED AND THIRTY FOUR ONLY

Drawn against shipment of 20 cartons of Cashmere Coats from Guangzhou to New York for collection

To ARRON FERER & SONS CO.
909 ABBOTT DRIVE DMAHA
MEBRASKA 68102 USA

For and on behalf of
GUANGDONG IMP. & EXP. CORPORATION
____
Authorized Signature (s)

ACCEPTED
28th, Mar., 2003
Payable at Bank of America
For ARRON FERER & SONS CO.
________________ Signature

（2）汇票二

Exchange for USD60 234.00　　Guangzhou, 20th, Mar., 2003

D/A At 30 days from sight of this First bill of exchange (Second unpaid)

Pay to the order of Construction Bank of China

the sum of US DOLLARS SIXTY THOUSAND TWO HUNDRED AND THIRTY FOUR ONLY

Drawn against shipment of 20 cartons of Cashmere Coats from Guangzhou to New York for collection

To ARRON FERER & SONS CO.
909 ABBOTT DRIVE DMAHA
MEBRASKA 68102 USA

For and on behalf of
GUANGDONG IMP. & EXP. CORPORATION
____
Authorized Signature (s)

ACCEPTED
28th, Mar., 2003
Payable at Bank of America
For ARRON FERER & SONS CO.
__________ Signature

(3) 汇票三

Exchange for USD60 234. 00 Guangzhou, 20th, Mar., 2003

D/A At 30 days after date of this First bill of exchange (Second unpaid)

Pay to the order of Construction Bank of China

the sum of US DOLLARS SIXTY THOUSAND TWO HUNDRED AND THIRTY FOUR ONLY

Drawn against shipment of 20 cartons of Cashmere Coats from Guangzhou to New York for collection

To ARRON FERER & SONS CO.
909 ABBOTT DRIVE DMAHA
MEBRASKA 68102 USA

For and on behalf of
GUANGDONG IMP. & EXP. CORPORATION

____
Authorized Signature (s)

ACCEPTED
28th, Mar., 2003
Payable at Bank of America
For ARRON FERER & SONS CO.
________________ Signature

(4) 汇票四

Exchange for USD60 234. 00 Guangzhou, 20th, Mar., 2003

D/A At 60 days after date of this First bill of exchange (Second unpaid)

Pay to the order of Construction Bank of China

the sum of US DOLLARS SIXTY THOUSAND TWO HUNDRED AND THIRTY FOUR ONLY

Drawn against shipment of 20 cartons of Cashmere Coats from Guangzhou to New York for collection

To ARRON FERER & SONS CO.
909 ABBOTT DRIVE DMAHA
MEBRASKA 68102 USA

For and on behalf of
GUANGDONG IMP. & EXP. CORPORATION

____
Authorized Signature (s)

ACCEPTED
28th, Mar., 2003
Payable at Bank of America
For ARRON FERER & SONS CO.
________________ Signature

(5) 汇票五

Exchange for USD60 234. 00 Guangzhou, 20th, Mar., 2003

D/A At one and half a month after date of this First bill of exchange (Second unpaid)

Pay to the order of Construction Bank of China

the sum of US DOLLARS SIXTY THOUSAND TWO HUNDRED AND THIRTY FOUR ONLY

Drawn against shipment of 20 cartons of Cashmere Coats from Guangzhou to New York for collection

To ARRON FERER & SONS CO.
909 ABBOTT DRIVE DMAHA
MEBRASKA 68102 USA

For and on behalf of
GUANGDONG IMP. & EXP. CORPORATION

____
Authorized Signature (s)

ACCEPTED
28th, Mar., 2003
Payable at Bank of America
For ARRON FERER & SONS CO.
________________ Signature

	汇票的付款期限	到期日
汇票一		
汇票二		
汇票三		
汇票四		
汇票五		

5. 汇票的背书

（1）根据汇票的收款人写法判断下列汇票转让时是否需要背书。按照下列所给条件将需要背书汇票的背书写在表格中。

收款人将汇票记名背书转让给 D Company，D Company 空白背书转让给 E Company，E Company 交付转让给 F Company，F Company 限制背书转让给 G Company。假设收款人公司有权签字人为李华，D Company 有权签字人为 John，E Company 有权签字人为 Mary，F Company 有权签字人为 Annie。

收款人写法	第一次转让	第二次转让	第三次转让	第四次转让
Pay to the order of A Company				
Pay to bearer				
Pay to A Company only				

（2）一笔托收业务中，出口公司为广州市 A 公司，有权签字人是张品，托收行是中国工商银行广东省分行，有权签字人是李源，代收行是美国花旗银行，进口公司是美国 B 公司。

① 汇票以出口公司为抬头人，收款公司空白背书给托收行，托收行记名背书给代收行。

Exchange for USD49 271.00	Guangzhou, 2nd, Oct., 2003
At * * * * * * sight pay to ________________ or order	
the sum of ________________	
To B Company New York	For: A Company, Guangzhou, China ________________ Authorized Signature (s)

汇票背面

② 汇票以托收行为抬头人，托收行记名背书给代收行。

Exchange for USD49 271.00	Guangzhou, 2nd, Oct., 2003
At ＊＊＊＊＊＊ sight pay to ______ or order	
the sum of ______	
To B Company New York	For: A Company, Guangzhou, China Authorized Signature (s)

汇票背面

6. 汇票的承兑

汇票收款人 A Company 委托银行向汇票付款人 B Company London 提示汇票承兑时，付款人根据所给条件在汇票上进行承兑，银行审核承兑汇票。

（1）付款人于 3 月 26 日在汇票左面作出普通承兑。

	Exchange for USD428 314.00 Shanghai, 16th, Mar., 2003 At 60 days after sight pay to the order of A Company the sum of Four Hundred Twenty Eight Thousand Three Hundred and Fourteen US dollars	
	To B Company London	For C Company, Guangzhou, China Authorized Signature (s)

（2）付款人于 3 月 26 日在汇票左面作出有条件承兑，条件为“货物抵达目的地付款”。

	Exchange for USD428 314.00 Shanghai, 16th, Mar., 2003 At 60 days after sight pay to the order of A Company the sum of Four Hundred Twenty Eight Thousand Three Hundred and Fourteen US dollars	
	To B Company London	For: C Company, Guangzhou, China Authorized Signature (s)

（3）付款人于3月26日在汇票左面作出部分承兑：仅付汇票金额的80%。

Exchange for USD428 314. 00　　Shanghai, 16th, Mar. , 2003
At 60 days after sight pay to the order of A Company
the sum of Four Hundred Twenty Eight Thousand
Three Hundred and Fourteen US dollars

To B Company
London

For C Company,
Guangzhou, China

Authorized Signature (s)

（4）付款人于3月26日在汇票左面作出承兑，指定由其账户行 Midland Bank 付款。

Exchange for USD428 314. 00　　Shanghai, 16th, Mar. , 2003
At 60 days after sight pay to the order of A Company
the sum of Four Hundred Twenty Eight Thousand
Three Hundred and Fourteen US dollars

To B Company
London

For C Company,
Guangzhou, China

Authorized Signature (s)

（5）付款人于3月26日在汇票左面作出承兑，延迟付款时间为“见票后90天付款”。

Exchange for USD428 314. 00　　Shanghai, 16th, Mar. , 2003
At 60 days after sight pay to the order of A Company
the sum of Four Hundred Twenty Eight Thousand
Three Hundred and Fourteen US dollars

To B Company
London

For C Company,
Guangzhou, China

Authorized Signature (s)

（6）Standard Chartered Bank Ltd. Hong Kong 于2003年11月26日承兑下面汇票后向 Bank of China Guangdong 填写并发出承兑通知书。

No. 11889/54

Exchange for HKD11 250. 00　　Guangzhou, 20th, November, 2003
At 30 days after sight pay to the order of Bank of China Guangdong
the sum of Eleven Thousand Two Hundred and Fifty HK dollars
Drawn under L/C No. 57833262 issued by Standard Chartered Bank Ltd.
dated 20th, Oct. , 2003

To Standard Chartered Bank Ltd.
Hong Kong

For Guangdong Imp& Exp Co.
Guangzhou

Authorized Signature (s)

STANDARD CHARTERED BANK LTD.

ACCEPTANCE NOTICE

To ______________________ Hong Kong, ____________

We give you below details of draft accepted by ourselves:

Your Ref No.	Drawer	Amount	Due	Remark

For Standard Chartered Bank Ltd.

Authorized Signature (s)

（二）本票

1. 客户向银行提交本票，按本票必要项目和所给问题对其进行审核和处理

（1）银行本票

Promissory Note for USD1, 000. 00 Boston, 4th, June, 2002

On demand we promise to pay to

the order of bearer

the sum of ONE THOUSAND US DOLLARS

Payable at Boston For First National Bank of Boston

Authorized Signature (s)

（2）商业本票

USD100, 000. 00 Haverty Furniture Companies

Atlanta 6th, Oct., 2002

AT SEVENTY DAYS AFTER DATE WE PROMISE TO PAY TO

THE ORDER OF BEARER

THE SUM OF ONE HUNDRED THOUSAND US DOLLARS

PAYABLE AT FULTON NATIONAL BANK, MAIN OFFICE, ATLANTA, GEORGIA

VALUE RECEIVED

DUE 15, Dec., 2002

HAVERTY FURNITURE CO.

Authorized Signature (s)

项目、问题 \ 类型	银行本票	商业本票
(1) 本票字样		
(2) 无条件支付承诺		
(3) 收款人名称		
(4) 付款人名称和付款地点		
(5) 出票地点和日期		
(6) 付款时间		
(7) 付款金额		
(8) 付款地点		
(9) 提示次数		
(10) 主债务人		

2. 根据所给条件填写本票

(1) Amount	£ 3, 026. 00
(2) Date and place of issue	8th/August/2003, Guangzhou, China
(3) Tenor	At 90 days after date
(4) Maker	Guangdong Imp. & Exp. Co., Guangzhou
(5) Payee	Chemicals Import & Export Company London

Promissory Note for ____________________
(Amount in figure)
____________________, ____________________, 200__
(Place and date of issue) (Name of month in letter)
On ____________________ against this promise note I (we) promise to
pay to ____________________ or order
the sum of ____________________
FOR VALUE RECEIVED ____________________
Payable at ____________________ ____________________
Signature (s) and full address of maker

(三) 支票

1. 客户向银行提交支票，按支票项目和所给问题对其进行审核和处理

Check No. 26 - 37 - 846 New York, 16th, Dec., 2003
Pay to the order of Toyota Company the sum of five thousand US dollars
USD5, 000 | 00
To Bank of New York For BBB Corp., New York
New York ____________________
Authorized Signature (s)

（1）支票字样	
（2）无条件支付命令	
（3）出票日期及出票地点	
（4）付款金额	
（5）付款期限	
（6）出票人	
（7）收款人	
（8）付款人	
（9）支票号码	
（10）提示次数	
（11）“Bank of New York，New York”与“BBB Corp.，New York”之间有何关系？	

2. 根据所给条件填写支票

（1）Drawer	Thames Enterprises Ltd.，London
（2）Drawee	The National Westminster Bank Ltd.，London
（3）Payee	Philips Hong Kong
（4）Date and place of issue	07/Jan./2001，London
（5）Amount	GBP79，014

Cheque No. 57931 ____________，____________ 200__

The National Westminster Bank Ltd.，London

Pay to

the order of ________________________________

the sum of ________________________________

GBP

For and on behalf of

____

Authorized Signature（s）

3. 根据所给条件在支票上划线

（1）出票人在支票上划线“Not Negotiable”。

（2）收款人在支票上特别划线，委托 Bank of East Asia，Guangzhou 做光票托收。

（3）Bank of East Asia，Guangzhou 在支票上再特别划线，委托 Bank of East Asia，New York 代收票款。

Check No. XXX

New York, 20th, Mar., 2002

AMERICAN EXPRESS BANK LTD.,

NEW YORK

Pay to

the order of AAA Company, Guangzhou

the sum of Six Thousand US Dollars

USD6,000	00

To American Express Bank Ltd.

New York

For and on behalf of

Funda Electricity Supply Co. Ltd.

Authorized Signature (s)

五、结果分析

1. 票据处理合法性分析。
2. 票据制作合规性分析。
3. 票据操作流程的准确与高效性分析。

实验二

汇款结算业务

一、实验目的

1. 汇款申请书填写完整、准确性的审核。

2. 根据汇款申请书和条件正确缮制汇款电文、信汇委托书、支付授权书、银行即期汇票。

3. 汇款指示完整、准确性的审核。

4. 掌握退汇和查询的处理。

5. 汇出汇款、汇入汇款业务处理流程。

6. 电汇、信汇、票汇业务处理流程。

二、实验原理

根据资金流向和结算工具流向是否相同，国际结算方式可划分为顺汇（Remittance）和逆汇（Reverse Remittance）。顺汇基本程序见图 2－1，逆汇基本程序见图 2－2。

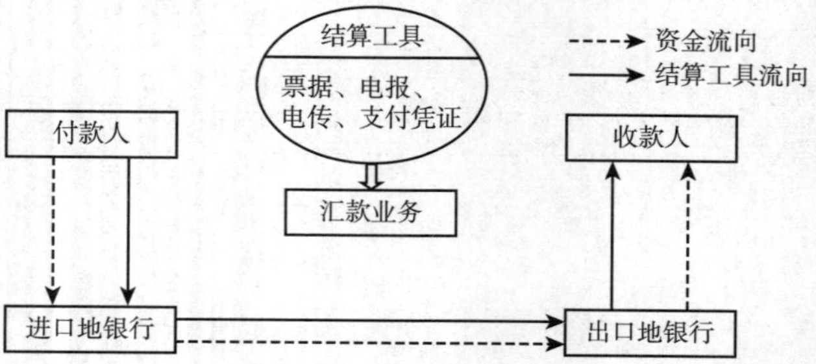

图 2－1　顺汇基本程序

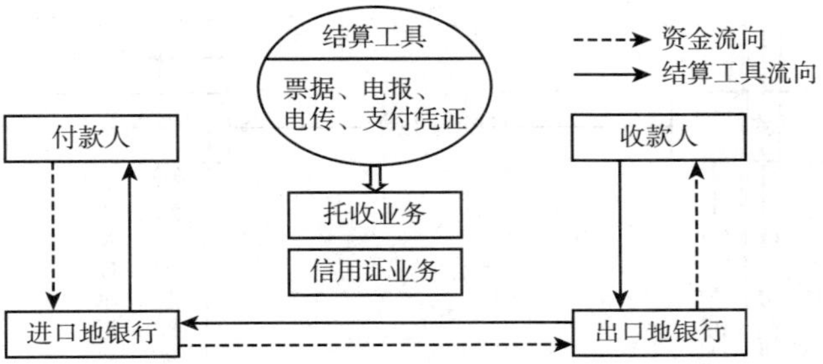

图 2 –2　逆汇基本程序

如图 2 –1 和图 2 –2 所示，顺汇可理解为付款人主动委托银行付款，包括汇款业务。逆汇可理解为收款人主动委托银行收款，包括托收业务和信用证业务。

在我国目前的外汇管理体制下，国际结算业务中涉及的外汇收付，必须按照外汇管理规定做好进口付汇核销和出口收汇核销。国际结算基本程序见图 2 –3。

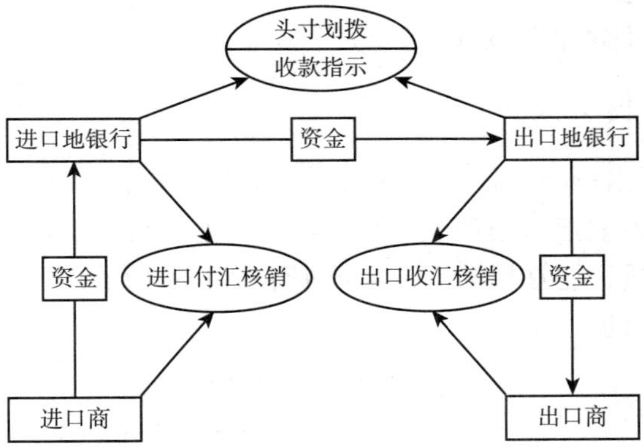

图 2 –3　国际结算基本程序

（一）汇出汇款业务知识点

汇款（Remittance）是指银行接受客户的委托，使用一定的结算工具，通过其在海外的分支机构或代理行，把款项付给国外收款人的一种结算方式。

以汇款操作程序划分，汇款业务包括汇出汇款业务和汇入汇款业务。

1. 汇出汇款业务（Outward Remittance）的处理

汇出汇款业务基本程序见图 2 –4。

电汇、信汇业务中汇出汇款环节包括：

① 汇款人填写电汇、信汇申请书，交款付费；

② 汇出行发出汇款指示。

票汇业务中汇出汇款环节包括：

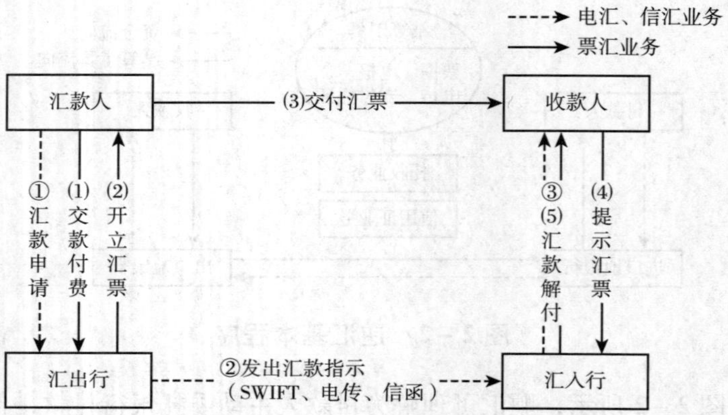

图 2-4　汇出汇款业务基本程序

（1）汇款人填写票汇申请书，交款付费；

（2）汇出行开出汇票；

（3）汇款人将汇票交付给收款人。

2. 汇款业务中的当事人

如图 2-5 所示，汇出行必须依据汇款人提交的汇款申请书处理汇出汇款业务，汇入行必须依据汇出行提交的汇款指示处理汇入汇款业务。汇出行应熟悉汇款申请书的内容并能对其填写的正确性进行审核，能够根据汇款申请书缮制汇款指示；汇入行必须熟悉汇款指示的内容并按照汇款指示要求进行处理。

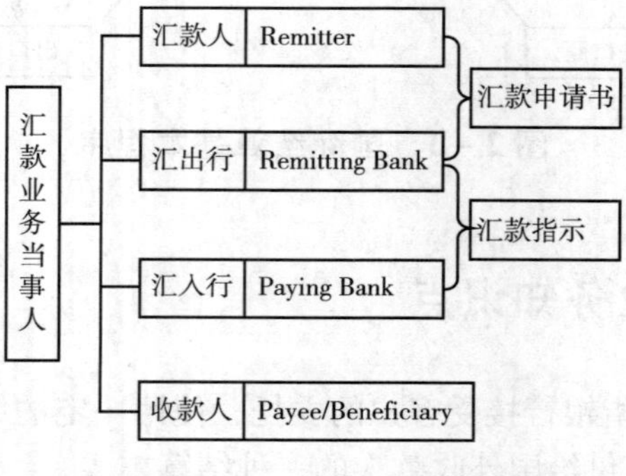

图 2-5　汇款业务当事人及关系

3. 汇出行业务处理环节和要求

汇款业务中，汇出行应按照汇款申请书的指示处理业务，在对汇款申请书填写正确性审核的基础上，向汇入行发送汇款指示，汇入行应按照汇款指示所示内容进行处理。汇出行业务处理环节和要求见图 2-6。

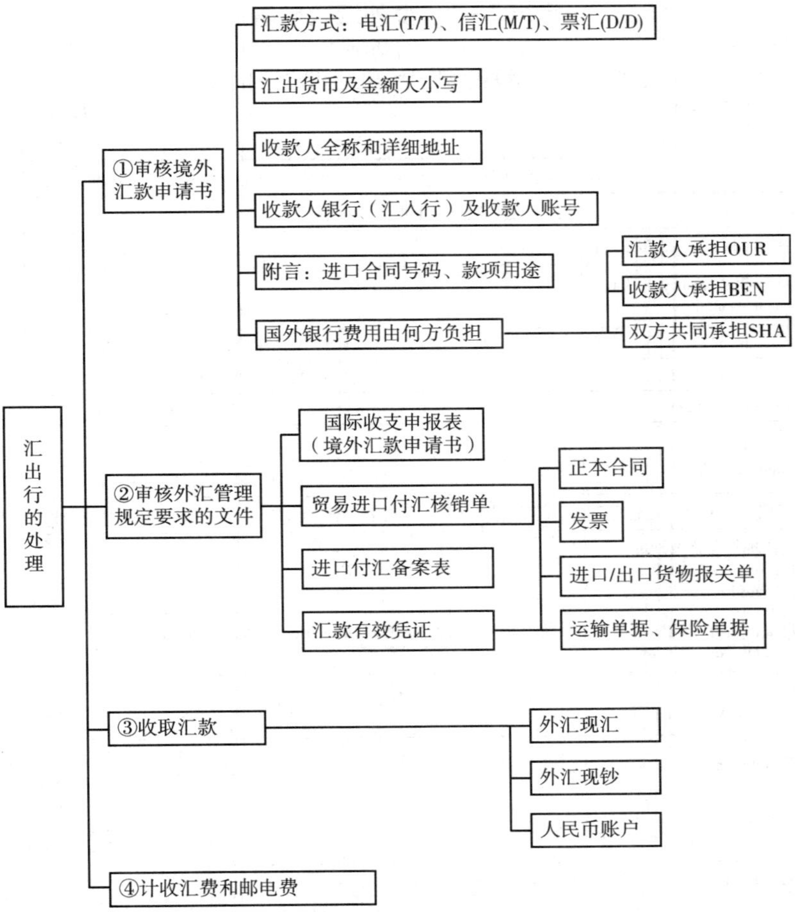

图 2－6　汇出行业务处理环节

4. 汇款申请书

2006 年，中国国家外汇管理局对国际收支申报系统进行了升级，统一了各行的境外汇款申请书格式。境外汇款申请书一式三联，分别为银行业务部门、汇款人和外汇局留存联。银行也可以根据实际需要，增加相应联数，如会计凭证联。

境外汇款申请书包括汇款人和银行填写两部分。汇款人需要填写的内容包括：汇款币种及金额、资金来源、账号、汇款人名称及地址、组织机构代码或个人身份证号码、收款人名称及地址、收款人开户银行、收款人账号、收款人国别、汇款费用的承担、交易附言及编码、合同号码、发票号码等信息。银行将汇款人填写的信息与其提交的商业单据和有效凭证进行核对无误后，办理售付汇手续，填写手续费、邮电费、使用的汇率等内容。境外汇款申请书见示样 2－1。

示样 2 -1　境外汇款申请书

致：Bank of China

To：

境外汇款申请书

APPLICANTION FOR FUNDS TRANSFERS (OVERSEAS)

日期

Date ________

		□电汇 T/T　□票汇 D/D　□信汇 M/T	发电等级	□普通 Normal　□加急 Urgent Priority
申报号码 BOP Reporting No.		□□□□□□　□□□□　□□　□□□□□□　□□□□		
20	银行业务编号 Bank Transac. Ref. No.		收点行/付款行 Receiver/Drawn on	
32A	汇款币种及金额 Currency & Interbank Settlement Amount		金额大写 Amount in Words	
其中	现汇金额 Amount in Fx		账号 Account No. /Credit Card No.	
	购汇金额 Amount of Purchase		账号 Account No. /Credit Card No.	
	其他金额 Amount of Others		账号 Account No. /Credit Card No.	
50a	汇款人名称及地址 Remitter's Name & Address		□对私	个人身份证号码 Individual ID No.
□对公	组织机构代码 Unit Code	□□□□□□□□-□		□中国居民个人 Resident Individual　□中国非居民个人 Non-Resident Individual
54/56a	收款银行之代理行名称及地址 Correspondent of Beneficiary's Bank Name & Address			
57a	收款人开户银行名称及地址 Beneficiary's Bank Name & Address	收款人开户银行在其代理行账号 Bene's Bank A/C No.		
59a	收款人名称及地址 Beneficiary's Name & Address	收款人账号 Bene's A/C No.		
70	汇款附言 Remittance Information	只限 140 个字位 Not Exceeding 140 Characters	71A	国内外费用承担 All Bank's Charges If Any Are To Be Borne By □汇款人 OUR　□收款人 BEN □共同 SHA
收款人常驻国家（地区）名称及代码 Resident Country/Region Name & Code				□□□
请选择：□预付货款 Advance Payment □货到付款 Payment Against Delivery □退款 Refund □其他 Others			最迟装运期	
交易编码 BOP Transac. Code	□□□□□□ □□□□□□	相应币种及金额 Currency &Amount	交易附言 Transac. Remark	
是否为进口核销项下付款		□是　□否	合同号	发票号
外汇局批件/备案表号			报关单经营单位代码	□□□□□□□□□□□□□
报关单号		报关单币种及总金额		本次核注金额
报关单号		报关单币种及总金额		本次核注金额

银行专用栏 For Bank Use Only		申请人签章 Applicant's Signature	银行签章 Bank's Signature
购汇汇率 Rate		请按照贵行背页所列条款代办以上汇款并进行申报 Please Effect The Upwards Remittance. Subject to The Condition Overleaf：	
等值人民币 RMB Equivalent			
手续费 Commission			
电报费 Cable Charges			
合计 Total Charges		申请人姓名 Name of Applicant 电话 Phone No.	核准人签字 Authorized Person 日期 Date
支付费用方式 In Payment of the Remittance	□现金 by Cash □支票 by Check □账户 from Account		
核印 Sig. Ver		经办 Maker	复核 Checker

填写前请仔细阅读各联背面条款及填报说明

Please read the conditions and instructions overleaf before filling in this application

汇款申请书（背面条款）

Application for Funds Transfer

条件和条款 Terms and Conditions

1. 申请人应仔细审阅申请书所列之各项条款内容。如因填写错误或字迹不清而引起的迟付或错付款，银行不承担责任。
All funds transfer should be checked carefully by the Applicant in each case and full in all the details in each proper blank space. The bank shall not be liable for any delayed payment or incorrect payment caused by the wrong information given or unclear writing.

2. 除非另有其他书面约定：
Unless it is otherwise expressly agreed to in writing：
(a) 银行将以邮件、电报、有线电报、无线电报、电报技术或电传等划款方式或汇票（此后均统一为讯息）发式进行划款，且银行可以使用明确的语言代码或密码来传送同该划款有关的任何讯息。
The Bank will transfer the funds by means of a mail telegram, cablegram, wireless, telegraphy or telex transfer or a draft (hereinafter collectively referred to as the message) and the Bank may send any message relative to this transfer in explicit language code or cipher.
(b) 尽管兑换及划款日期应完全由银行自主决定，银行通常将在其从申请人处收到款项的当天按银行收到款项当天的银行现行汇率把款项兑换成外汇并划出。
The Bank will normally convert into foreign values and transfer the funds on the day the funds are received by it from the Applicant at the Bank's prevailing rate on the day such funds are received by the Bank though the date of conversation and transfer are entirely at the Bank's discretion.

3. 银行完成兑换及划款的书面申明应是终局性的。
The bank's statement in writing that it has effected such conversion and transfer shall be conclusive.

4. 银行可以代表申请人使用任何代理行、代理人或分代理人。本申请书和有关文件可以传送至银行的任何分行，并由其处理。
The bank may use on behalf of the Applicant any correspondent or agent or sub-agent. The application and its related documents can be transmitted to and processed by any of the Bank' branches.

5. 如果付款以受款国以外的货币表示，该款项仍可按银行代理行或分代理行的现行买入价，以汇出国货币支付给收款人，除非收款人按其与银行的代理行或代理人或分代理人之间的安排，在支付所有与此有关的银行的代理行、代理人或分代理人的费用后，获得某些其他货币的付款。
If payment is expressed in a currency other than that of the country to which the funds are to be sent, the funds shall nevertheless be payable to the payee in the currency of the country where the remittance is sent at the Bank's correspondent agent or sub-agent prevailing buying rate unless the payee by arrangement with the Bank's correspondent or agent or sub-agent obtains payment in some other currency upon paying all charges of the Bank's correspondent or agent or sub-agent in connection therewith.

6. 在任何情况下，申请人均认可款项的发送应完全由申请人承担各方面的风险且因不应被认为对下列事项负责：讯息传送过程中可能发生的或因其对讯息错误理解而产生的或在任何邮件、电报、有线电报、无线电报、电报技术或电传公司收到后产生的或因银行的代理行或代理人或分代理人或上述机构的任何雇员造成的或由于银行，其代理行货代理人或分代理人直接控制以外的任何其他原因造成的任何残缺、中断、遗漏、疏忽、违约、错误与延误。
In all circumstances the Applicant acknowledges that the funds are sent entirely at the Applicant's own risk in every respect and the Bank is not held liable for any mutilation, interruption omission, error neglect, default, mistake or delay which may occur in the transmission of the message or from which tits misinterpretation on or after receipt on the part of any mail telegram, cablegram wireless, telegraphy or telex company or by the Bank's correspondent or agent or sub-agent or any employee of the aforesaid or through any other cause beyond the direct control of the Bank, its correspondent or agent or sub-agent.

7. 如经申请人请求且仅在银行已收到有效的取消付款通知后，银行可向申请人退款，且在款项已经兑换的情况下，退款应在按退款当天的银行买入价计算并减去银行的开支及其代理行或代理人的开支后方能进行。
A refunds may be made by the Bank to the Applicant if requested by the Applicant but only if and after the Bank has received notice of effective cancellation of the payment of the funds, and in the case of funds already converted, a refund is only to be mad calculated at the Bank's buying rate on the day the refund is made less the Bank's expenses and that of its correspondent or agent or sub-agent.

8. 如果汇票、邮件划款或其他讯息遗失时，申请人在第二次签发汇票、邮件划款或其他讯息来取代第一次讯息前将被要求签署一份赔偿书。
In event of the loss of a draft, mail transfer or other message, the Applicant will be required to sign a letter of indemnity before the issue of a second draft, mail transfer or other message in place of the first one.

9. 申请人同意支付与执行申请人的指令有关的银行佣金以及一切其他收费，并在适用法律许可的范围内支付相关的印花税。
The Applicant agrees to pay the Bank's commission and all other charges in connection with the carrying out of the Applicant's instructions and pay the relevant stamp duty to the extent permitted by applicable law.

10. 本“汇款申请书”及其条件以中英文两种文字写成，两种文本如有不一致，以中文本为准。
This Application for Funds Transfer and its terms and conditions are made both in English and Chinese languages, if there is any discrepancy between both versions, the Chinese version shall prevail.

5. 汇款种类和汇款指示

汇款的种类见图 2-7。

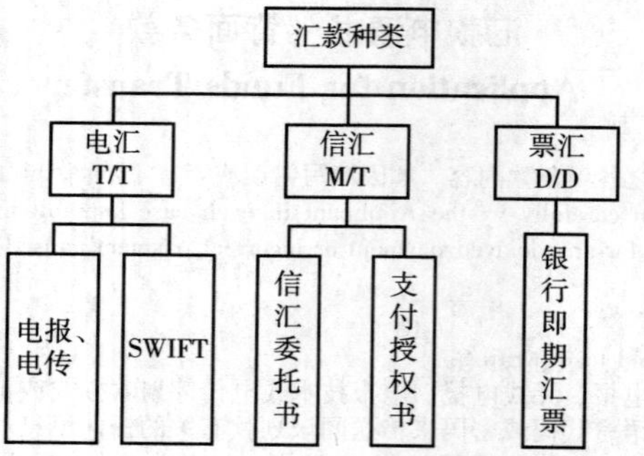

图 2-7 汇款的种类

如图 2-7 所示，汇款业务包括电汇（Telegraphic Transfer，T/T），信汇（Mail Transfer，M/T），票汇（Remittance by Bank's Demand Draft，D/D）。电汇、信汇业务处理程序比较相似，票汇业务中因采用银行即期汇票作为结算工具，增加了汇票处理中的提示操作过程。

(1) 电汇业务的基本程序和汇款电文

① 电汇业务基本程序

电汇业务基本程序见图 2-8。

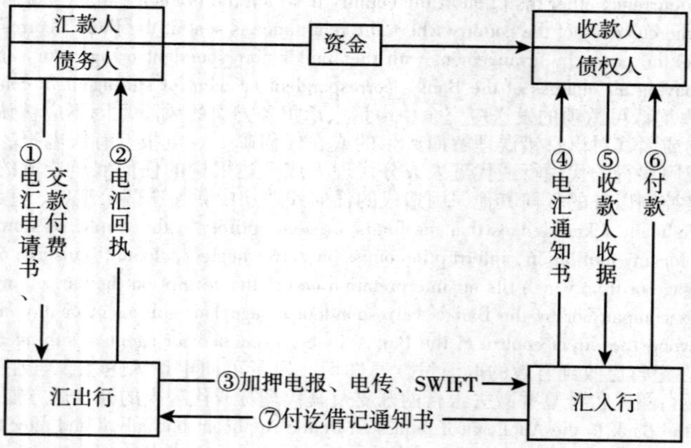

图 2-8 电汇业务基本程序

② 采用电报或电传的汇款格式

汇款指示中电报或电传格式见示样 2-2。

示样 2－2　电报或电传格式

FM：（汇出行名称） TO：（汇入行名称） DATE：（发电日期） TEST（密押）　　OUR REF NO. ________（汇款编号） NO ANY CHARGES FOR US（我行不负担费用） PAY ___(AMT)___ （付款金额）VALUE (DATE)（起息时间）TO (BENEFICIARY)___（收款人） MESSAGE ________（附言） ORDER ________（汇款人名称） COVER ________（头寸划拨指示）

③采用 SWIFT 的汇款格式

适用于汇款的 SWIFT 格式、名称及用途见表 2－1。

表 2－1　适用于汇款的 SWIFT 格式

报文格式	MT 格式名称	名称描述
MT103	客户汇款	请求调拨资金
MT200	单笔金融机构头寸调拨至发报行自己账户	请求将发报行的头寸调拨至其他金融机构的该行账户上
MT201	多笔金融机构头寸调拨到它自己的账户上	多笔 MT200
MT202	单笔普通金融机构头寸调拨	请求在金融机构之间的头寸调拨
MT203	多笔普通金融机构头寸调拨	多笔 MT202
MT204	金融市场直接借记电文	用于向 SWIFT 会员银行索款
MT205	金融机构头寸调拨执行	国内转汇请求
MT210	收款通知	通知收报行，它将收到头寸记在发报行账户上

其中 MT103 客户汇款的基本格式见表 2－2。

表 2－2　MT103 格式

Status	Tag	Field Name
M	20	Sender's reference
O	13C	Time Indication
M	23B	Bank Operation Code
O	23E	Instruction Code
O	26T	Transaction Type Code
M	32A	Value date/Currency code/Interbank Settled amount
O	33B	Currency/Instructed Amount
O	36	Exchange Rate
M	50a/k	Ordering customer

续表

Status	Tag	Field Name
O	51A	Sender's Correspondent
O	52a/d	Ordering Institution
O	53a/b/d	Sender's Correspondent
O	54a/b/d	Receiver's Correspondent
O	55a/b/d	Third Reimbursement Institution
O	56a/b/d	Intermediary Institution
O	57a/b/d	Account with Institution
M	59	Beneficiary Customer
O	70	Remittance Information
M	71A	Details of Charges
O	71F	Sender's Charges
O	71G	Receiver's Charges
O	72	Sender to Receiver Information
O	77B	Regulatory Reporting
O	77T	Envelope Contents

M = Mandatory field 指令区

O = Optional field 选择区

(2) 信汇业务的基本程序和信汇委托书、支付授权书

① 信汇业务基本程序

信汇业务基本程序见图 2－9。

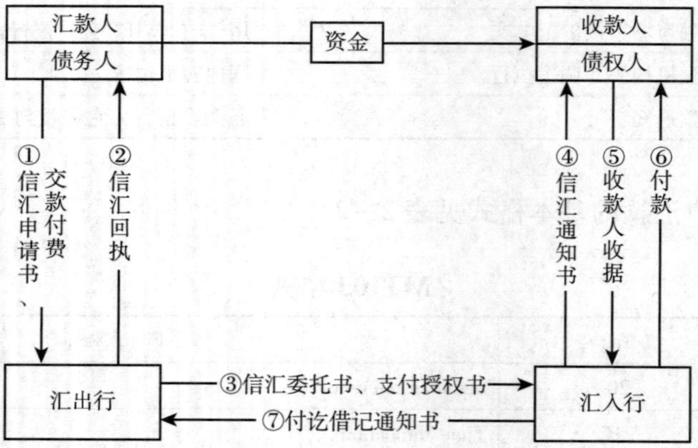

图 2－9　信汇业务基本程序

② 信汇委托书（Mail Transfer Advice）与支付委托书（Payment Order）

信汇委托书（Mail Transfer Advice）见示样 2－3，支付委托书（Payment Order）见示样 2－4。

示样 2 -3　信汇委托书

中国银行广州分行

BANK OF CHINA, GUANGZHOU BRANCH

Mail Transfer Advice

下列汇款，请即解付，如有费用请内扣。我已贷记你行账户。

Please advise and effect the following payment less your charges if any. In cover, we have CREDITED your A/C with

日期 Date: ______, ________, ____________

Guangzhou

此致
TO

信汇号码 No. of Mail transfer	收款人 To be paid to	金额 Amount

大写金额

Amount in Words: ____

附言

Message

汇款人

By order of ____

中国银行广州分行

BANK OF CHINA, GUANGZHOU BRANCH

示样 2 -4　支付委托书

中国银行支付委托书

BANK OF CHINA

PAYMENT ORDER

Guangzhou

Date: ______, ________, ____________

此致
TO

信汇号码 No. of payment order	收款人 To be paid or credited to	金额 Amount

大写金额

Amount in words: ____

汇款人

By order of ____

附言

Remarks

□You are authorized to debit our account with you

□We have credited your A/C with us.

中国银行广州分行

BANK OF CHINA, GUANGZHOU BRANCH

(3) 票汇业务的基本程序和银行即期汇票

① 票汇业务基本程序

票汇业务基本程序见图 2 -10。

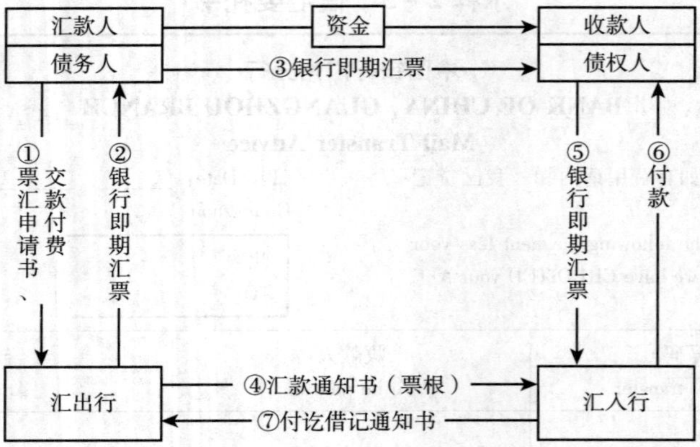

图 2－10　票汇业务基本程序

② 银行即期汇票（Banker's Demand Draft）

票汇中的银行即期汇票（Banker's Demand Draft）见示样 2－5。实务中，为方便货币清算，一般采用中心汇票汇款，即汇出行开立即期汇票的付款人是汇票上所用货币结算中心的银行。如一张以英镑为面值的汇票上的付款行是英镑清算中心所在地伦敦的一家银行，这就是一张英镑中心汇票。

示样 2－5　银行即期汇票

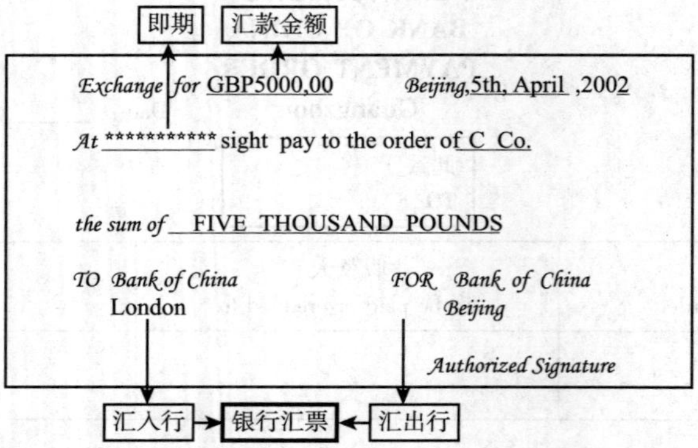

6. 汇款头寸的调拨

汇款人一般委托自己的账户行作为汇出行，汇出行在汇款指示中应结合与汇入行之间开立账户方式的不同，写明汇款头寸划拨指示。如果汇出行和汇入行是账户行关系，汇款头寸划拨则通过汇出行贷记汇入行存款账户或汇入行借记汇出行存款账户进行。如果汇出行和汇入行之间没有直接开立存款账户，则要通过其他银行转账划拨头寸。汇款头寸调拨见图 2－11。

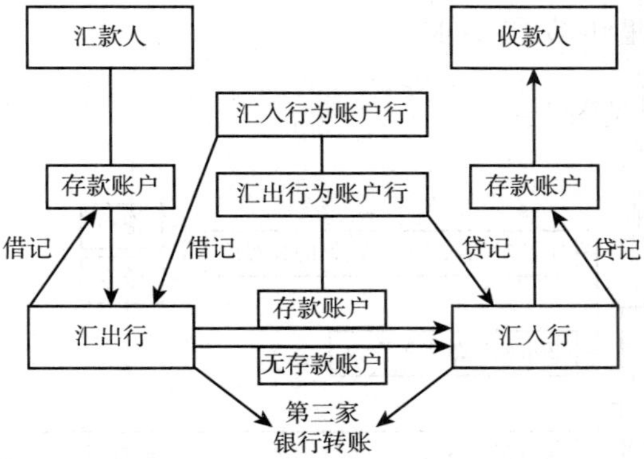

图 2－11　汇款头寸的划拨指示

（二）汇入汇款业务知识点

1. 汇入汇款业务（Inward Remittance）的处理

汇入汇款基本程序见图 2－12。

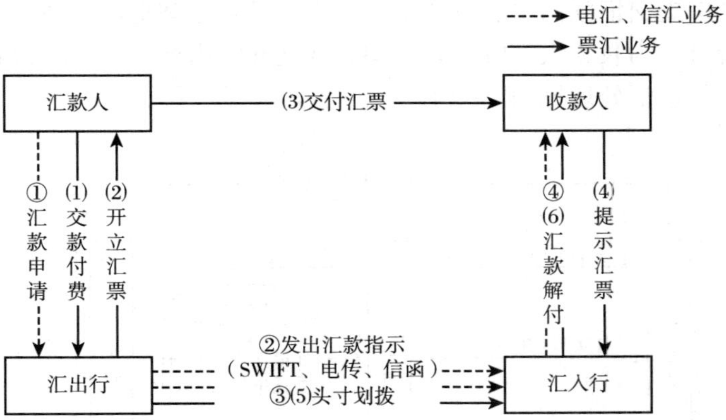

图 2－12　汇入汇款业务基本程序

电汇、信汇业务中汇入汇款环节包括：
② 汇入行收到汇款指示；
③ 头寸划拨；
④ 汇款解付。
票汇业务中汇入汇款环节包括：
（4）收款人提示汇票；
（5）头寸划拨；
（6）汇款解付。

2. 汇入行业务处理环节和要求

汇入行业务处理环节见图 2－13。

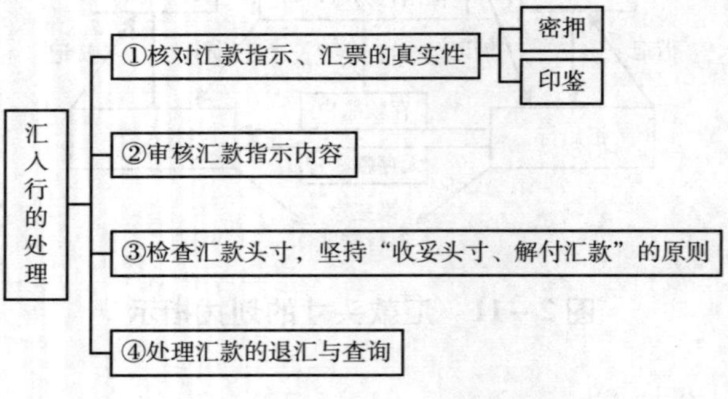

图 2－13　汇入行处理环节

3. 汇款业务中的退汇

退汇指汇款人和收款人中某一方在汇款解付前要求银行撤销该笔汇款业务。如果是汇款人提出办理退汇，应提交汇款回单、收费单至汇出行柜台办理退汇申请手续；如果是收款人提出退汇，汇入行可作为收款人拒收汇款处理，并通知汇出行，由汇款人到汇出行办理退汇手续。汇款业务中的退汇处理见图 2－14。

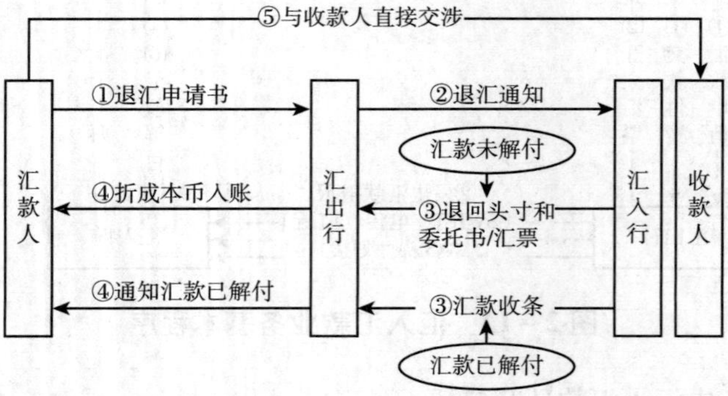

图 2－14　汇款的退汇处理

办理票汇退汇时，为避免挂失汇票找到后而导致银行承担风险，汇款人应向汇出行出具担保书。担保书格式见示样 2－6。

示样 2－6　担保书

LETTER OF INDEMNITY

WHEREAS YOU ISSUED TO ME/US A DRAFT NO. ________ DATED ________ FOR THE AMOUNT OF ________ IN FAVOUR OF ________ AND WHEREAS SUCH DRAFT HAS BEEN LOST OR MISLAID, AND I/WE HEREBY REQUEST YOU TO ISSUE TO ME/US A REPLACEMENT DRAFT.

NOW THEREFORE IN CONSIDERATION OF THE PAYMENT OF THE AMOUNT OF SUCH DRAFT, I/WE HEREBY UNDERTAKE AND AGREE TO INDEMNITY YOU AND YOUR AGENTS FROM AND AGAINST ALL LOSS WHICH YOU/THEY MAY INCURE OR SUSTAIN BY ANY REASON, AND PARTICULARLY IN THE EVENT OF SUCH DRAFT BEING PRESENTED AND PAID, I/WE AGREE TO REPAY YOU THE AMOUNT SO PAID ON SUCH DRAFT AND FUTHER, IF SUCH DRAFT SHALL AT ANY TIME HEREAFTER COME TO MY/OUR POSSESSION, I/WE WILL DELIVER TO YOU WITHOUT ANY COST.

三、实验内容

1. 作为汇出行审查汇款申请书的填写。
2. 作为汇出行根据所给汇款申请书缮制电汇业务中汇款电报。
3. 作为汇出行根据所给汇款申请书缮制 SWIFT 格式下汇款电文。
4. 作为汇入行审查汇款电文。
5. 作为汇出行缮制信汇业务中信汇委托书。
6. 作为汇入行审查信汇业务中支付授权书。
7. 作为汇入行审查票汇中的银行即期汇票。
8. 作为汇出行、汇入行审查、处理退汇电文和退汇通知书。
9. 作为汇出行、汇入行审查、处理查询电文和查询书。

四、实验步骤

（一）汇款申请书

2010 年 6 月 4 日，CHINA NAT. METALS & MINERALS I/E CORP. 向中国银行提交下面这张境外汇款申请书，汇出行按所给问题审核汇款申请书。

Date 2010 年 6 月 4 日

√□电汇 T/T □票汇 D/D □信汇 M/T	发电等级	√□普通 Normal	□加急 Urgent Priority

申报号码 BOP Reporting No.		□□□□□□□ □□□□ □□ □□□□□□□ □□□□		
20	银行业务编号 Bank Transac. Ref. No.		收点行/付款行 Receiver/Drawn on	
32A	汇款币种及金额 Currency & Inter-bank Settlement Amount	HK Dollars 20, 000. 00	金额大写 Amount in Words	HK Dollar Twenty Thousand only
其中	现汇金额 Amount in Fx	HK Dollars 20, 000. 00	账号 Account No. /Credit Card No.	3456989674
其中	购汇金额 Amount of Purchase		账号 Account No. /Credit Card No.	
其中	其他金额 Amount of Others		账号 Account No. /Credit Card No.	
50a	汇款人名称及地址 Remitter's Name & Address	CHINA NAT. METALS & MINERALS I/E CORP.	个人身份证号码 Individual ID No.	
√□对公	组织机构代码 Unit Code □□□□□□□□-□	□对私	□中国居民个人 Resident Individual	□中国非居民个人 Non-Resident Individual
54/56a	收款银行之代理行名称及地址 Correspondent of Beneficiary's Bank Name & Address			
57a	收款人开户银行名称及地址 Beneficiary's Bank Name & Address	收款人开户银行在其代理行账号 Bene's Bank A/C No. PO SANG BANK LTD. HongKong		
59a	收款人名称及地址 Beneficiary's Name & Address	收款人账号 Bene's A/C No. 0709166060322-8 United Trading Company Hong Kong		
70	汇款附言 Remittance Information	只限 140 个字位 Not Exceeding 140 Characters COMM. UNDER S/C NO. CT0011-01	71A	国内外费用承担 All Bank's Charges If Any Are To Be Borne By √□汇款人 OUR □收款人 BEN □共同 SHA

收款人常驻国家（地区）名称及代码 Resident Country/Region Name & Code					□□□
请选择：□预付货款 Advance Payment □货到付款 Payment Against Delivery □退款 Refund □其他 Others				最迟装运期	
交易编码 BOP Transac. Code	□□□□□□ □□□□□□	相应币种及金额 Currency &Amount		交易附言 Transac. Remark	
是否为进口核销项下付款	□是 □ 否	合同号		发票号	
外汇局批件/备案表号			报关单经营单位代码	□□□□□□□□□□□□□	
报关单号		报关单币种及总金额		本次核注金额	
报关单号		报关单币种及总金额		本次核注金额	

银行专用栏 For Bank Use Only		申请人签章 Applicant's Signature	银行签章 Bank's Signature
购汇汇率 Rate		请按照贵行背页所列条款代办以上汇款并进行申报 Please Effect The Upwards Remittance. Subject to The Condition Overleaf:	
等值人民币 RMB Equivalent			
手续费 Commission			
电报费 Cable Charges			
合计 Total Charges		申请人姓名 张青 Name of Applicant 电话 Phone No.	核准人签字 Authorized Person 日期 Date
支付费用方式 In Payment of the Remittance	□现金 by Cash □支票 by Check □账户 from Account		
核印 Sig. Ver		经办 Maker	复核 Checker

(1) 汇款方式	
(2) 汇款人公司名称	
(3) 收款人公司名称、地址	
(4) 汇款金额	
(5) 款项用途	
(6) 银行费用由哪方支付?	
(7) 汇款当日港币现钞价为 86.77/87.80，港币现汇价为 87.47/87.8，汇款人应提交多少人民币现钞给银行?	
(8) 银行在哪些情况下可免责?	
(9) 在我国现行外汇管理规定下，汇款人办理汇款业务时应注意哪些事项?	

（二）电汇中的汇款电文

1. 将下面三份电文的内容填写在表格中。

（1）电文一

FM：HONGKONG AND SHANGHAI BANKING CORPORATION LTD. HONG KONG
TO：THE AGRICULTURAL BANK OF CHINA GUANGZHOU
DATE：8TH JUNE
TEST 2876A OUR REF TT200498
PLS PAY HKD34000. VALUE 8 JUNE TO ACCOUNT NO. 764583934-128 FAVOUR PRECISION PHOTO EQUIPMENT LTD. JINXING BUILDING 22 GUANGZHOU MESSAGE COMM. UNDER S/C NO. 87364 ORDER AA CO. COVER WE HAVE CREDITED YOUR ACCOUNT WITH US.

（2）电文二

BKCH CN BJ 400
103
CITIUS33
20：0307DR09888762
23B：CRED
32A：090511 USD2376，
33B：USD2376，
50K：AAA COMPANY
59：/3765498
BBB COMPANY
SHA

（3）电文三

FM：BANK OF AMERICA，NEW YORK
TO：INDUSTRIAL AND COMMERCIAL BANK OF CHINA，GUANGDONG BRANCH
DATE：14TH，OCT
TEST 87593 OUR REF TT10908 - 04
PLS PAY USD38000. VALUE 14，OCT. TO GUANGDONG CEREALS OIL N FOODSTUFFS I/E GROUP CORP. VIA A/C NO. 310910079 BEING PROCEEDS UNDER S/C NO. CT89768 ORDER WIN FOOD CO. LTD. COVER CREDITED YOUR H. O. ACCOUNT

电文 审核内容	电文一	电文二	电文三
(1) 汇出行			
(2) 汇入行			
(3) 发电日期			
(4) 密押、汇款编号			
(5) 汇款金额、起息时间			
(6) 收款人			
(7) 附言			
(8) 汇款人			
(9) 头寸划拨			

2. 中国农业银行广州市分行接受 CHINA NAT. METALS & MINERALS I/E CORP. 的汇款申请，于 2003 年 3 月 8 日发送汇款电文。其中，汇入行是 PO SANG BANK LTD.，HONG KONG，汇出行在汇入行开立有港币存款账户，费用由受益人承担。

FM：________________________

TO：________________________

DATE ____________

TEST：____________ OUR REF NO. ____________

NO ANY CHARGES FOR US

PAY ____________ VALUE ____________ TO ____________

____________ FOR CREDITING ACCOUNT NO. ____________

MESSAGE ________________________

ORDER ________________________

COVER ________________________

3. 中国农业银行广州市分行采用 SWIFTM/T103 汇款格式，将电报内容输入电脑发送至汇入行 PO SANG BANK LTD.，HONG KONG。

（三）信汇中的委托书和支付授权书

1. 汇出行 Industrial and Commercial Bank of China, Shangdong 根据业务内容，填写支付授权书。

①Date：15th，Sept.，2002；②Paying Bank：Hongkong and Shanghai Banking Corp. Ltd.，Hong Kong；③Ref No.：MT28376；④Amount：HKD30，000.00；⑤Cover：Please debit our A/C with you；⑥Message：Commission under S/C NO. FB9768；⑦Payee：Win Food Company，Ltd.，Hong Kong；⑧Remitter：Shangdong Cereals Oil & Foodstuffs I&E Group Corp.

Industrial and Commercial Bank of China

Shangdong

PAYMENT ORDER

Date：____，____，____

TO

No. of payment order	To be paid or credited to	Amount

Amount in words：________________

By order of ________________ Remarks

☐You are authorized to debit our account with you.

☐We have credited your A/C with us.

☐Funds remitted to you via.

Industrial and Commercial Bank of China

2. 1999 年 3 月 18 日，中国银行广州分行收到中国银行香港分行信汇委托书，中国银行广州分行按信汇委托书所示内容对其进行审核。

中国银行香港分行

BANK OF CHINA，HONG KONG BRANCH

下列汇款，请即解付，如有费用请内扣。我已贷记你行账户。

Please advise and effect the following payment less your charges if any. In cover，we have credited your account with us.

日期 15，March，1999，Guangzhou

此致

TO BANK OF CHINA，GUANGZHOU

信汇号码 No. of Mail transfer	收款人 To be paid to	金额 Amount
MT992568	Ruiqi Garment Co. Ltd.，Guangzhou a/c No. 34568-113	HKD200，000.

大写金额

Amount in Words：H. K. Dollars Two Hundred Thousand

附言：

Message：Being Proceeds under S/C No. 99CC03026

汇款人

By order of

Universal Garment Imp. & Exp. Co.

Hong Kong

中国银行香港分行

BANK OF CHINA，HONG KONG

(1) 汇出行	
(2) 汇入行	
(3) 收款人	
(4) 汇款人	
(5) 汇款货币及金额	
(6) 款项用途	
(7) 汇款头寸划拨指示	

(四) 票汇中的银行即期汇票

中国银行纽约分行于 2002 年 6 月 1 日收到 Wiletecc Co. , Ltd. , New York 提交的汇票，按所给问题对汇票进行审核和处理。

BANK OF CHINA

This draft is valid for one
year from the date of Issue

No.1256679
Amount USD20,000.00
Guangzhou, 15th, May, 2002

中国银行

Pay to the order of Wiletecc Co., Ltd., New York
the sum of U.S. Dollars Twenty Thousand Only

To Bank of China
410 Madison Avenue
New York
110017

BANK OF CHINA
GUANGZHOU

(1) 汇出行	
(2) 汇入行	
(3) 收款人	
(4) 汇款人	
(5) 汇款货币及金额	
(6) 汇票的付款期限	
(7) 客户提出汇票遗失，出票行应如何处理?	
(8) 是否是中心汇票?	

（五）汇款中的退汇

根据汇出行和汇入行发出的退汇电文和退汇通知书，按其所示内容进行处理。

1. 退汇电文一

> We return herewith your Draft No. C249/7681 for USD200, 000.00 for credit to our account 786 - 723987 - 023 Anglo International Co. and regret to advise that we are unable to deposit the proceeds to the captioned account because the name of the payee differs from our records. It should read as Anglo International Co. Ltd....

2. 退汇电文二

> Our Draft No. 3893 - 987 dated 20 May 2002 for AUD105, 000.00 for credit to Good luck Co. Ltd., referring to the captioned item, we are informed by the remitter that the above mentioned draft has gone ashtray in mail delivery.
>
> In this connection, we shall be much obliged if you will cancel the said draft from your records and return the relative advice of drawing to us.

3. 退汇通知书

> Your Remittance receipt No. TT56343
> for HKD65, 000.00 dated Aug. 30, 2001
> payable to A/C No. 86754
> for A/C of BBB Co.
> with reference to the above, we return herewith the remittance receipt to you for the following reason (s):
> ☐ No account
> ☒ Account closed
> ☐ Name and A/C not matched
> ☐ Insufficient detail to identify
> Kindly acknowledge receipt by signing and returning to us the attached copy of this letter.

业务及处理	退汇电文一	退汇电文二	退汇通知书
(1) 汇款基本情况			
(2) 退汇理由			
(3) 退汇的银行			
(4) 银行的处理			

（六）汇款的查询

根据汇出行和汇入行所给查询电文和查询书，按其所示内容进行处理。

1. 电文一

Re: Our P. O. Ref H783746 Dated Feb. 20, 2000

The beneficiary claims non-receipt of the funds up to date, you are kindly requested to investigate this matter and revert by telex.

2. 电文二

Re: Our P. O. Ref 8976224 Dated July 10, 2001

Please furnish us with more information such as contract No., the name of the goods and the quantity, because the beneficiary are unable to apply with the information given.

3. 电文三

Re: Our P. O. Ref J67398 Dated Nov. 18, 2001

Please let us learn the full address of the payee of your above payment order, as we have been unable to locate them and are holding your order pending.

4. 电文四

Re: Our P. O. Ref 563765 Dated Jan. 7, 2000

If the payment has already been effected, please forward us the payee's receipt.

5. 查询书一

XXX Bank

To: YYY Bank

Our ~~DD~~/~~MT~~/TT No. TT200498 dated 8th June 2002 for USD505, 000.

in favor of Kim Hwa Textiles Co., 89 London St., Singapore

We refer to the above remittance and request you to take note of the following item (s) marked "X" and act accordingly:

☐ We have received your letter/cable dated.

☐ The name and address of the payee are amended to read as follow:

☒ The remitter has informed us that the above remittance had not yet been received by the payee up to the date.

☐ If the payment has already been effected, please forward the payee's receipt to us.

☒ Kindly confirm to us by ~~mail~~/cable/the date of payment of the remittance.

☐ The above DD has been return to us for cancellation.

☐ The above DD has been reported lost and should be treated as cancelled, please confirm that you have placed stop payment on this DD.

☐ At the request of the remitter please cancel the above remittance immediately, if unpaid and credit the amount to our account with you after deducting your charges if any, under advice to us.

XXX Bank

6. 查询书二

XXX Bank

To: YYY Bank

Re: Your TT999888 dated 990323 for USD8 900. Payable to Hing Long Magnetronic Co. Ltd.

We refer to the above mentioned item and would like to advise you as marked "X" below:

☐ The payment order is not properly signed, please confirm its regularity.

☒ The amount in words and figures on the payment order differ, please confirm the correct amount.

☐ Payment was effected on ________, a photocopy of the beneficiary's receipt is enclosed for your reference.

☐ The beneficiary cannot be located at the address given, please give further information.

☐ Name/address of the beneficiary is incomplete, please give full details.

☐ Beneficiary's name/account number does not match with that in our records.

Please furnish us with the correct information. (The account name/number should read ________.)

☐ The beneficiary's name differs from that in his/her identification document please let us have the correct name.

☒ We do not appear to have received your reimbursement, please promptly investigate and credit our account with Bank of America N. T. &S. A., in settlement under advice to us.

☐ We enclose a photocopy of telex from ________ of ________ with yourselves, please authenticate it.

☐ We have not yet received your reply to our letter (s) of ________, photocopy (ies) of which is/are endorsed for your reference. Please let us have your reply as soon as possible.

☐ Please contact our Miss/Mr. ________ of remittance Dept at ________.

☐ With reference to your letter dated ________ claiming non-receipt of our debit advice of the above remittance, we hereby enclose the duplicated advice for your disposal.

Thank you for your kind attention.

XXX Bank

查询 / 问题	电文一	电文二	电文三	电文四	查询书一	查询书二
查询内容						
银行的处理						

五、结果分析

1. 汇款申请书填写的完整性与准确性分析。
2. 汇款指示缮制的正确性与明确性分析。
3. 电汇、信汇、票汇操作流程的准确与高效性分析。

实验三

托收结算业务

一、实验目的

1. 托收委托书填写完整、准确性的审核。
2. 根据托收委托书和条件正确缮制托收指示。
3. 托收指示完整、准确性的审核。
4. 掌握拒付中退票通知书、拒付电文的发送、审核和处理。
5. 跟单托收处理流程。
6. 付款交单、承兑交单处理流程。
7. 掌握 URC522 对托收业务处理中的规定。

二、实验原理

(一) 出口托收业务知识点

1. 托收业务 (Collection) 的处理

托收是指委托人向银行提交凭以收取款项的金融票据或商业单据或两者兼有，要求托收行通过其联行或代理行或提示行向付款人请其付款的一种结算方式。

按托收业务处理程序划分，托收业务包括出口托收(Outward Collection) 和进口代收(Inward Collection)。按是否附带全套商业单据划分，托收业务包括光票托收(Clean Collection) 和跟单托收(Documentary Collection)，国际贸易结算中跟单托收较为常见。跟单托收基本程序见图 3－1。

如图 3－1 所示，出口托收业务环节包括：

① 进、出口商签订买卖合同，采用托收结算业务；

② 出口商装船发货，取得提单，制作或准备好其他单据；

③ 出口商填写托收委托书（有的银行又称托收申请书），向银行提交跟单汇票；

④ 出口商取得回执；

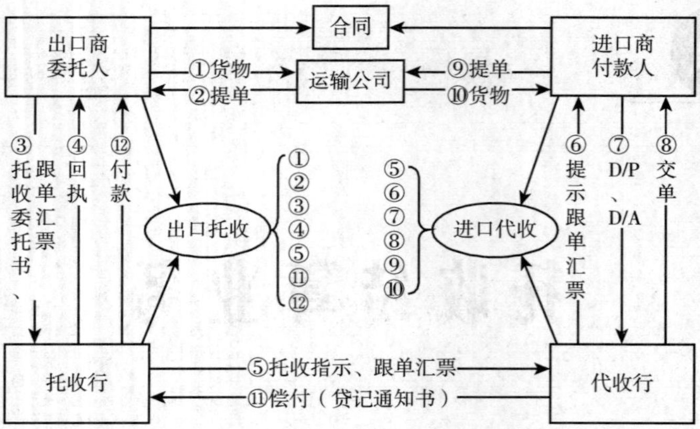

图 3－1　跟单托收业务基本程序

⑤ 托收行向代收行发出托收指示和邮寄跟单汇票；
⑪ 托收行收到代收行发出的贷记通知书；
⑫ 托收行贷记出口商存款账户。
进口代收业务环节包括：
⑤ 代收行检查、核对托收指示和跟单汇票；
⑥ 代收行向付款人提示跟单汇票；
⑦ 付款人付款或承兑汇票；
⑧ 代收行向付款人交单；
⑨ 进口商向轮船公司提交提单；
⑩ 进口商取得货物；
⑪ 代收行通知托收行承兑/付款，发出贷记通知书。

2. 托收业务中的当事人

如图 3－2 所示，托收业务作为一种委托代理业务，委托人与托收行应按托收委托书指示处理，托收行与代收行应按托收指示处理。此外，托收业务各方当事人还应严格按托收统一规则（URC522）规定办理。跟单托收指示一般为一式多联，其中正、副联寄代收行，回单联交委托人，银行留底联（含会计凭证）供托收行内部使用。跟单托收委托书见示样 3－1，跟单托收指示见示样 3－2。

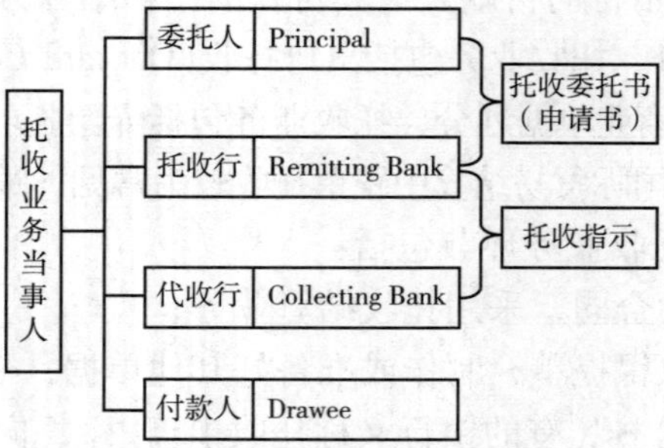

图 3－2　托收业务当事人

示样 3－1　跟单托收委托书

跟单托收委托书（正面）

致：中国银行广州分行

TO：BANK OF CHINA GUANGZHOU BRANCH

We hand the under mentioned item for disposal in accordance with the following instructions and subject to the terms and conditions set out overleaf for

Original Collection Application

Date：15th，Nov.，2003

兹送上下列文件，请按照下述指示办理，本司并同意遵照背面之条款。

[X] COLLECTION 代收

☐ NEGOTIATION under Documentary Credit 议付信用证下单据

☐ Please advance against the bill/documents 请予垫款

[X] Please do not made any advance 无须垫款

Please mark 请填上下列文件的份数

Number of DOCUMENTS ATTACHED　　我司账号 Our A/C No.　0201107－365－7681

Draft 汇票	Bill of lading 提单	Airway bill 空运单	Cargo Receipt 货物收据	Invoice 发票		Memo. 中旅社承运收据	Cert. Of Qual/Quan. 品质/数量证明书	Cert. Of Origin 产地证明书	Ins. Pol/Cert. 保险单/证书	Packing List 装箱单	Weight List 重量单	Bene. Cert. 受益人证明书	Cable Copy 电报副本
				Comm.	Cust.								
2/2	3/3			2/2			1/1	1/1					

OTHER DOCUMENTS 其他文件

DRAWEE 付款人 Good Luck Company，Hongkong

ISSUING BANK 开证银行	DOCUMENTARY CREDIT NO. 信用证编号
TENOR 期限 30 DAYS SIGHT DRAFT NO./DATE 票号/日期 13th，Nov.，2003	DRAFT AMOUNT 金额 US ＄527，360.00

FOR "BILLS NOT UNDER L/C" PLEASE FOLLOW INSTRUCTIONS MARKED "X" 如属非信用证下单据请按下列有 X 之条办理

Deliver documents against ~~PAYMENT~~/ACCEPTANCE　~~付款~~/承兑交单

☐Acceptance/ payment may be deferred pending arrival of carrying vessel　货到后方承兑/交款

Collection charges outside Guangzhou for account of Drawee　外埠代收手续费付款人负担

Please collect interest at 6% p. a. from Drawee　请向付款人按年息 6% 厘计收利息

☐Please waived interest/charges [X] Do not waive interest/charges　如拒付利息/手续费 ~~可免收~~/不可免收

if refuse in the event of dishonor　如付款人拒绝承兑或付款

Please warehouse and insure goods for our account　请将各货物入仓投足保险，各项费用由我司负责

[X] Please do not protest ☐Protest　请不须/~~需~~作拒绝承兑/付款证书

[X] Advise dishonor by ☐Airmail [X] Cable　若未兑付请以~~航邮~~/电报通知

☐ In case of need refer to

Who will assist you to obtain acceptance/payment but who has no authority to amend the terms of the bill

该司会协助贵行取得承兑/付款但无权更改任何条款

☐Designated Collecting Bank（if any）：指定代收银行

PAYMENT INSTRUCTIONS

请将款项收我司账号

X Please credit proceeds to our A/C No. 0201107－365－7681

其他☐ Others

OTHER INSTRUCTIONS 其他指示

如有查询，请洽我司。In case of any questions，please contact our Mr./Miss　　Tel No.

For：Guangdong Arts & Craft Imp. & Exp. Company

Authorized Signature（s）负责人签字

跟单托收委托书（背面）

TERMS AND CONDITIONS：

We agree as follows：

1. We undertake to indemnity you and keep you indemnified against：

(a) all liabilities, losses, damages, costs, expenses, claims and demands which you may incur or sustain by reason of your acts, omissions, delays, defaults or negligence in respect of any or all of the matters herein, including all legal and other costs and expenses (on a full indemnity basis) which you may incur in connection with your dealings with any issuing or reimbursing bank under the LC and the enforcement, or attempted enforcement of your rights hereunder;

(b) any loss incurred by you as a result of (i) the payment of any amount by you to issuing or reimbursing bank under Clause 1 (d) above being in a currency other than that in which such amount is payable by us hereunder, and (ii) any variation having occurred in the rates of exchange between the date as at which the amount payable by us is converted into such other currency and the date of actual payment by us to you.

2. We agree that the undertakings and agreements contained herein are in addition and without prejudice, to any other security or securities which you may at or subsequently hold, and are not affected by any intermediate payment or settlement of account or settlement under the LC. You may at anytime and without reference to us give up, deal with, vary, exchange or abstain from performing or enforcing any other security or the LC at any time and discharge any party to it, and realize it or any of them as you think fit.

3. All draft and/or documents not payable at your office are sent to you for transmission at our risk alone and in particular without responsibility on your part for any act, neglect, default, failure or insolvency of any correspondent, agent or sub-agents or for any loss or delay arising in the course of transmission. They may be transmitted by mail or any other means, be routed directly or circuitously through any of your branches, correspondents, agents or sub-agents. Further they may be transmitted to the drawee, maker or paying agent for payment in cash, credit or for acceptance or certification.

4. Collections are subject to our rules and regulations for the time being in force, and to those of your correspondents, agents, sub-agents and the laws of any country concerned.

5. Notwithstanding any provisions herein, we hereby waive presentment, demand, protest and notice of dishonor of the draft and/or documents, NO delay or omission on your part in exercising any right, power, privilege or remedy in respect of these undertakings and agreements shall impair such right, power, privilege or remedy or be construed as a waiver of it nor shall any single or partial exercise of any such right, power, privilege or remedy. The rights, powers, privileges and remedies provided herein and indemnity are cumulative and not exclusive of any rights, powers, privileges or remedies provided by law.

6. You will exercise due diligence in the selection of your agents. However, for the event we designate a correspondent other than the one of our own selection you will follow our instructions upon the explicit understanding that we assume and confirm all the acts of such correspondent of our own choice and agree to hold you harmless from all consequences thereof.

示样 3－2　跟单托收指示

The Industrial & Commercial Bank of China

Collection Instruction

To:	ORIGINAL

Dear Sirs,　　　　Date ________________

Our Ref No. ________________

We send you herewith the under-mentioned item（s）/documents for collection

Drawer:	Draft No.: Date:	Due Date/Tenor
Drawee（s）:	Amount:	
Goods:	From	To
By par	On	

Documents	Draft	Invoice	B/L	Ins. Policy/Cert.	W/M	C/O			
1st									
2nd									

Please follow instructions marked "X":

☐Deliver documents against payment/acceptance.

☐Remit the proceeds by airmail/cable.

☐Airmail/cable advice of payment/acceptance.

☐Collect charges outside ________________ from drawer/drawee.

☐Collect interest for delay in payment ________________ days after sight at ________________% P. A.

☐Airmail /cable advice of non-payment/non-acceptance with reasons.

☐Protest for non-payment/non-acceptance.

☐Protest waived.

☐When accepted, please advise us giving due date.

☐When collected, please credit our account with ________________.

☐Please collect and remit proceeds to ________________ Bank for credit our account with them under their advice to us.

☐Please collect proceeds and authorize us by airmail/cable to debit your account with us.

Special Instructions　　　　For Industrial & Commercial Bank of China

This collection is subject to
Uniform Rules for Collection
(1995 Revision) ICC Publication No. 522

____

Authorized Signature（s）

3. 托收行业务处理环节和要求

托收行业务处理环节和要求见图3－3。

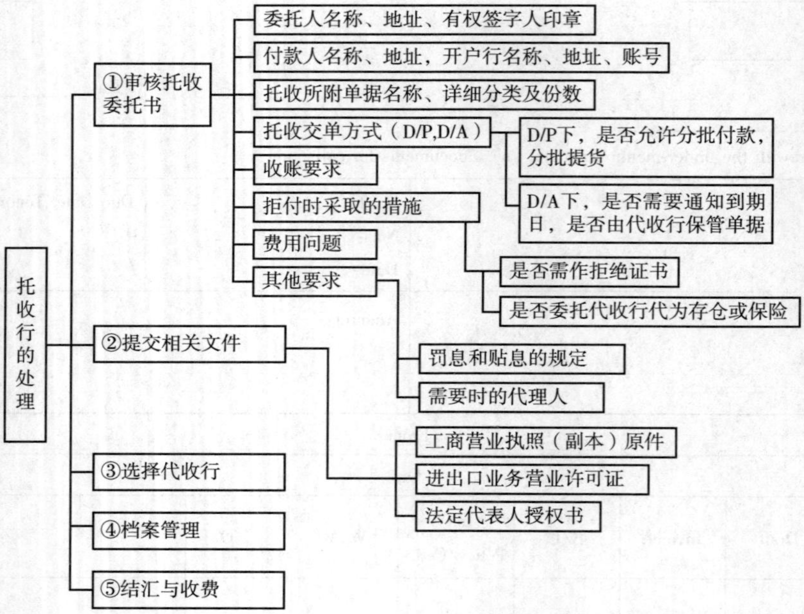

图3－3　托收行业务处理环节

4. 跟单托收的交单条件

跟单托收包括付款交单（Documents against Payment，D/P）和承兑交单（Documents against Acceptance，D/A）。付款交单中根据委托人提交汇票期限不同，分为即期付款交单（D/P at sight）和远期付款交单（D/P at xx days after sight）。不同交单条件仅对代收行与付款人之间的处理产生影响，委托人与托收行、托收行与代收行之间的处理不受交单条件的影响。即期付款交单基本程序见图3－4，远期付款交单基本程序见图3－5，承兑交单基本程序见图3－6。

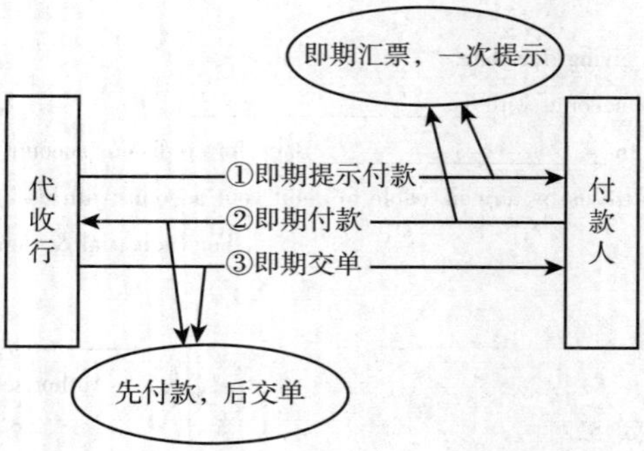

图3－4　即期付款交单基本程序

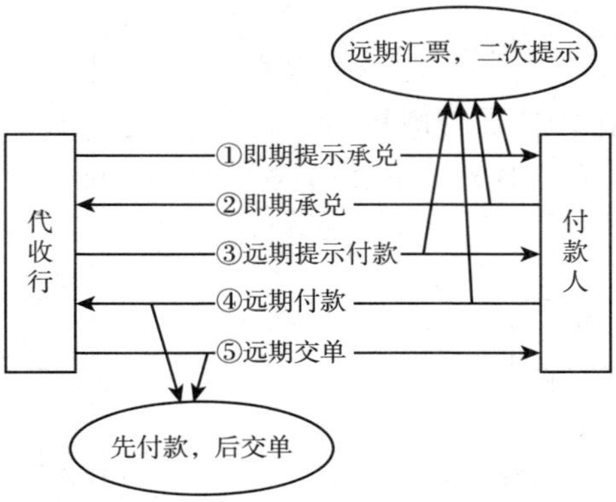

图 3 -5　远期付款交单基本程序

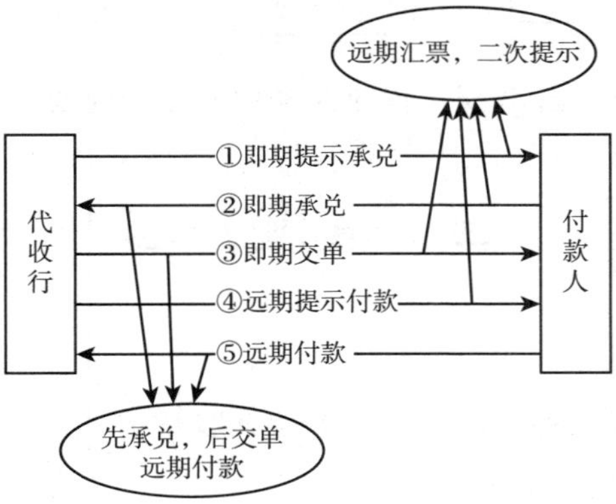

图 3 -6　承兑交单基本程序

（二）进口代收业务知识点

1．代收行业务处理环节和要求

代收行业务处理环节和要求见图 3 -7。

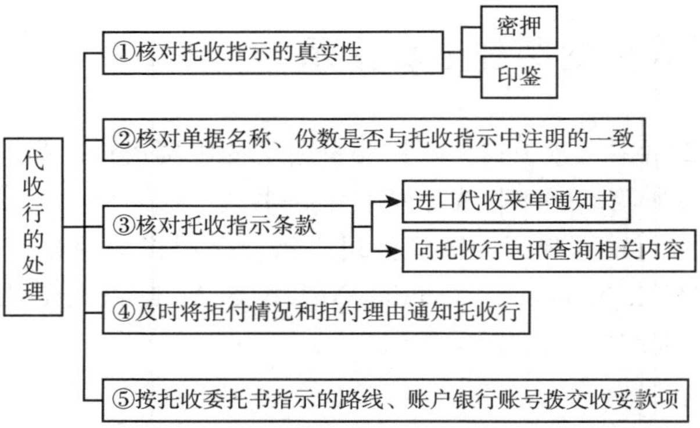

图 3 -7　代收行业务处理环节

2. 进口代收中的拒付（Dishonour）

代收行向付款人提示跟单汇票后遭拒付，应按托收指示要求及时发出退票通知或拒绝证书。URC522 第二十六条 C 款对拒付处理规定了 60 天的期限。代收业务中拒付处理见图 3－8。

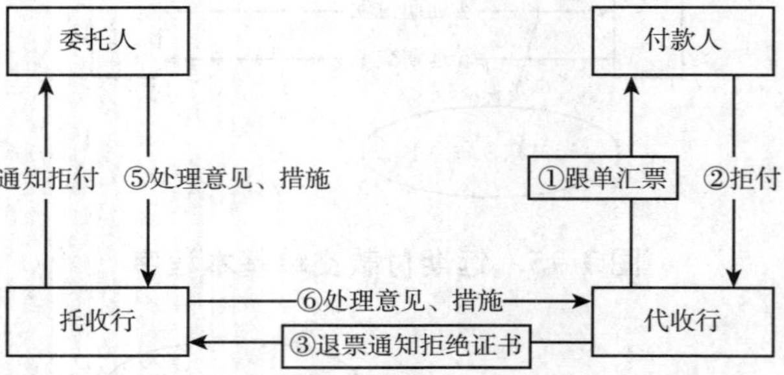

图 3－8　代收业务中的拒付处理

三、实验内容

1. 托收行审核光票托收委托书。
2. 托收行根据所给光票托收委托书缮制光票托收指示。
3. 托收行审核跟单托收委托书。
4. 托收行根据所给跟单托收委托书缮制跟单托收指示。
5. 代收行审核跟单托收指示。
6. 代收行缮制和发送退票通知、拒付电文。
7. 托收行对收到的退票通知和拒付电文进行审核和处理。

四、实验步骤

（一）光票托收中的委托书和指示

1. 2003 年 5 月 22 日中国进出口公司广州分公司向中国银行广州分行提交下面这张光票托收委托书，托收行按所给问题审核光票托收委托书。

2. 中国银行广州分行根据中国进出口公司广州分公司提交的光票托收委托书，于 2003 年 5 月 23 日缮制并向代收行 Bank of America N. T. & S. A. 邮寄光票托收指示，并选择第二项、第三项、第五项、第六项托收指示条款。

中国银行

票据托收委托书

委托日期：22/05/2003

票据种类 Items	号码 Original No.	出票日期 Date of Issue	币别及金额 Currency& Amount
支票	7838	14/05/2003	US $ 2000. 00
付款人	Bank of America N. T. & S. A.		
出票人	AAA Trading Company, New York		
受益人	China National Imp. & Exp. Corp., Guangzhou		
开户账号 A/C No.	098730 - 9867 - 9423	银行编号 Ref No.	CC09176

[X] 款项收妥后，请付我账。

[X] 你行及国外行所有托收费用，请付我账。

中国进出口公司广州分公司

(1) 委托人公司名称	
(2) 付款人公司名称	
(3) 托收金额	
(4) 托收票据种类、内容	
(5) 银行费用由哪方支付？	
(6) 光票托收适用范围	
(7) 托收行是否承担必定收回票款的责任？	
(8) 托收行办理托收业务的依据是什么？	
(9) 哪些票据或凭证可提交给银行办理光票托收？	

中国银行 分行

BANK OF CHINA

ORIGINAL

In all correspondence
Please always quote

OUR REF 384CC-28975

Date：

敬启者：

致 TO

Dear Sirs，

兹奉下列票据，请即收我册。

We have pleasure in forwarding the following cheque/draft for payment /collection.

票据号码 Original No.	付款人 Drawn on	出票人 Drawer	金额 Amount
TOTAL AMOUNT			

Please follow instructions below （marked X）：

☐Credit the proceeds immediately under usual reserves.

☐Collections subject to final payment Not under usual reserves.

☐CREDIT the proceeds （ less your charges，if any） to our US Dollar account with you under authenticated telex/SWIFT advice to us quoting our Ref No.

☐REMIT the proceeds （less your charges， if any） to our account with ____________ via CHIPS ____________ under their authenticated telex/SWIFT advice to ____________ Quoting our Ref No. ____________

☐If unpaid please cable advise us and return the same cheque/draft to us by registered airmail with reason （s） of non-payment.

☐Please acknowledge receipt.

Unless otherwise expressly stated herein，this collection is subject to the“UNIFORM RULES FOR COLLECTION” -I. C. C. BROCHURE522.

For：BANK OF CHINA GUANGZHOU

____

Authorized Signature （s）

（二）跟单托收中的委托书和指示

1. 2003 年 5 月 18 日 Guangdong Arts & Craft Imp. & Exp. Company 向中国银行广州分行提交下面这张跟单托收委托书，托收行按所给问题审核跟单托收委托书。

托收委托书

致：中国银行广州分行
TO：BANK OF CHINA GUANGZHOU
We hand the under mentioned item for disposal in accordance with the following instructions and subject to the terms and conditions set out overleaf for

Original Collection Application
Date：18th，May，2003
兹送上下列文件，请按照下述指示办理，本司并同意遵照背面之条款。

[X] COLLECTION 代收
☐ NEGOTIATION under Documentary Credit 议付信用证下单据

[X] Please advance against the bill/documents 请予垫款
☐ Please do not made any advance 无须垫款

Please mark 请填上下列文件的份数
Number of DOCUMENTS ATTACHED 我司账号 Our A/C No. 87364－752－9251

Draft 汇票	Bill of lading 提单	Airway bill 空运单	Cargo Receipt 货物收据	Invoice 发票 Comm.	Invoice 发票 Cust.	Memo. 中旅社承运收据	Cert. Of Qual/Quan. 品质/数量证明书	Cert. Of Origin 产地证明书	Ins. Pol/Cert. 保险单/证书	Packing List 装箱单	Weight List 重量单	Bene. Cert. 受益人证明书	Cable Copy 电报副本
2/2	4/4			2/2			1/1	1/1		1/1			

OTHER DOCUMENTS 其他文件

DRAWEE 付款人 Good Luck Company，Hongkong

ISSUING BANK 开证银行 | DOCUMENTARY CREDIT NO. 信用证编号

TENOR 期限 AT SIGHT DRAFT NO./DATE 票号/日期 18th，May | DRAFT AMOUNT 金额 HK $ 625,450.00

FOR “BILLS NOT UNDER L/C” PLEASE FOLLOW INSTRUCTIONS MARKED “X” 如属非信用证下单据请按下列有 X 之条办理

Deliver documents against PAYMENT/~~ACCEPTANCE~~ 付款/~~承兑交单~~

☐Acceptance/ payment may be deferred pending arrival of carrying vessel 货到后方承兑/交款

Collection charges outside Guangzhou for account of Drawee 外埠代收手续费付款人负担

Please collect interest at 5% p. a. from Drawee 请向付款人按年息 5% 厘计收利息

[X] Please waived interest/charges ☐ Do not waive interest/charges 如拒付利息/手续费可免收/~~不可免收~~
if refuse in the event of dishonor 如付款人拒绝承兑或付款

Please warehouse and insure goods for our account 请将各货物入仓投足保险，各项费用由我司负责

[X] Please do not protest ☐Protest 请不须/~~即做~~拒绝承兑/付款证书

[X] Advise dishonor by ☐Airmail [X] Cable 若未兑付请以~~航邮~~/电报通知

[X] In case of need refer to A Trading Co.，Hong Kong Who will assist you to obtain acceptance/payment but who has no authority to amend the terms of the bill 该司会协助贵行取得承兑/付款但无权更改任何条款

[X] Designated Collecting Bank（if any）：指定代收银行 Standard Chartered Bank Ltd.，Hong Kong

PAYMENT INSTRUCTIONS
请将款项收我司账号
[X] Please credit proceeds to our A/C No. 87364－752－9251
其他☐ Others

OTHER INSTRUCTIONS 其他指示
如有查询，请洽我司。In case of any questions，please contact our Mr./Miss 王江 Tel No. 35678765

For：Guangdong Arts & Craft Imp. & Exp. Company

Authorized Signature（s）负责人签字

(1) 委托人公司名称、账号	
(2) 付款人公司名称	
(3) 指定代收行	
(4) 托收金额、付款期限	
(5) 托收单据种类、份数	
(6) 银行费用由哪方支付?	
(7) 交单条件	
(8) 利息支付情况	
(9) 拒付时是否需发出退票通知?	
(10) 拒付时是否需出具拒绝证书?	
(11) 需要时的代理人及作用是什么?	
(12) 托收行邮寄单据遗失时，是否需承担责任?	

2. 中国银行广州分行根据 Guangdong Arts & Craft Imp. & Exp. Company 提交的跟单托收委托书，于 2003 年 5 月 20 日缮制并向代收行 Standard Chartered Bank Ltd., Hong Kong 邮寄跟单托收指示，其中：①Ten boxes of lamps from Guangzhou to Hong Kong by par of Tianyu vessel on May 12, 2003；②款项划至中国银行香港分行贷记托收行账户；③两次寄单。

中国银行

Bank of China

Office:

Address:

SWIFT/Telex:

Documentary Collection Order

ORIGINAL

Date:
Please always quote Our Ref No.: GuHPBK04401

Dear Sirs,

Our Ref No. ____________

We enclose the following documents for collection:

To (Collecting Bank):	Drawer:
Drawee:	Amount:
Invoice No.: FG898765-21	Due Date/Tenor:
Goods:	From To
By par	On

Documents	Draft	Invoice	B/L	Ins. Policy/Cert.	W/M	C/O			
1st									
2nd									

Please follow instructions marked "X":

☐Deliver documents against payment/acceptance.

☐Remit the proceeds by airmail/cable.

☐Airmail/cable advice of payment/acceptance.

☐Collect charges outside ____________ from drawer/drawee.

☐Collect interest for delay in payment ____________ days after sight at ____________% P. A.

☐Airmail /cable advice of non-payment/non-acceptance with reasons.

☐Protest for non-payment/non-acceptance.

☐Protest waived.

☐When accepted, please advise us giving due date.

☐When collected, please credit our account with ____________.

☐Please collect and remit proceeds to ____________ Bank for credit our account with them under their advice to us.

☐Please collect proceeds and authorize us by airmail/cable to debit your account with us.

Special Instructions

This collection is subject to

Uniform Rules for Collection

(1995 Revision) ICC Publication No. 522

For Bank of China

____

Authorized Signature (s)

3. 1999 年 9 月 30 日，中国银行广州分行收到汇丰银行香港分行邮寄的跟单托收委托书和跟单汇票一套，托收行根据所给问题审核托收指示。

中国汇丰银行　香港分行

HongKong and Shanghai Banking Corp. Ltd. Hong Kong Branch

Tlx:

Tel:

Fax:

Documentary Collection Order

ORIGINAL

In all correspondence please always quote

OUR REF 180C-09877

Date: 28th, Sept., 1999

TO: **Bank of China, Guangzhou**

Dear Sirs,

We enclose the following documents for collection:

Drawer: ARRON FERER & SONS CO. 909 ABBOTT DRIVE OMAHA NEBRASKA 68102	Drawer's No.	Due Date/Tenor	Amount:
Drawee: GUANGDONG PROVINCIAL IMP. & EXP. CORP.	N25 - 92X818	35days sight	USD66, 120. 00

Docu. sent by	Draft	Invoice Comm.	Invoice Cust.	Trspt Docu. Neg.	Trspt Docu. N/N	Ins. Pol/Cert.	Cert. Qly/Qty	Pkg. Wgt. List	C/O Form A.	Bene's Cert.
1st	1/2	2/3		3/3	1	2/2			2/2	
2nd	1/2	1/3								

Other Documents: Inspection Cert. 2/2

Covering Shipment of: 57 MT ZINC OXIDE 99.7% MIN

Please follow instructions marked "X":

[X] Deliver documents against ACCEPTANCE.

[X] In case of non-payment and /or non-acceptance please do not protest but advice us by cable stating reasons.

[X] In case of a time bill, please advise us by CABLE the date of maturity after acceptance.

[X] All your charges are to be born by DRAWEES.

□Collect interest from drawees at ____________% p. a. from date of draft to date of payment.

IN SETTLEMENT:

[X] Please remit the proceeds to Bank of America, New York, N. Y. by T/T for credit of our A/C No. 519 - 90171 with them CHIPS U. I. D. No. 315437 quoting our Ref No. under advice to us.

□Credit our account by T/T with

A/C No. UID No. under their tested telex advice to

quoting our Ref No. and your telex/airmail advice to us.

For HongKong and Shanghai Banking Corp. Ltd.
Hong Kong Branch

____

Authorized Signature (s)

（1）托收行	
（2）代收行	
（3）委托人公司	
（4）付款人公司	
（5）托收金额、付款期限	
（6）单据名称、份数	
（7）寄单次数和份数	
（8）交单条件和代收行的处理	
（9）拒付时代收行的处理	
（10）代收行的费用由谁支付？	
（11）承兑后，代收行是否应将到期日通知托收行？	
（12）代收行如何将收妥款项划入托收行账户？	

（三）托收中的拒付

托收行根据代收行发出的退票（拒付）通知书和拒付电文，按其所示内容进行处理。

1．退票通知书一

UNPAID ITEM MEMO 退票通知书 Date 日期______

To 退回 Bank No. 银行号码 Item No. 票据号码 Amount 金额

Returned for reason（s）marked"X" below 退票时请参阅下面画上 X 项目：

	1	Refer to drawer	请与持票人接洽
	2	Not arranged for	未经接洽
	3	Drawn against uncollected funds. Please present again	托收款项未收到，请再提示
	4	Account closed	此户已结清
	5	Insufficient funds	存款不足
X	6	Out of date	已经过期
	7	Post dated	票非即期
	8	Payment countermanded by the drawer	此票已停止支付
	9	Words and figures differ	金额文字与数码不符
	10	Amount in words required/incomplete/illegible	金额文字未写/不全/不清
	11	Alteration requires drawer's full chop/signature	涂改处需出票人盖注/签字
	12	Drawer's chop/signature differs from specimen in our possession	出票人图章/签字与本行存底不符
	13	Drawer's chop/signature required	出票人未签章/签字
	14	Drawer's chop/signature incomplete	出票人图章/签字不完全
	15	Date incomplete/illegible	出票日期不全/不明
	16	Endorsement irregular/illegible/missing/unknown	背书不妥/不清楚/遗失/不详
	17	No advice received	未接通知
X	18	Payee's/Banker's endorsement required	未经受款人/贵银行背书
	19		

Bank of China Hong Kong

____

Authorized Signature（s）

2. 退票通知书二

Canadian Imperial Bank of Commerce

Notice of Dishonor

To: YYY Bank

With reference to the captioned item, we wish to inform you that it has remained unaccepted/unpaid for the reason (s) marked "X" below:

☐ Drawee will accept/pay on arrival of goods.

☐ Drawee states that he is in negotiation with the drawer explaining the reasons for non-payment and /or non-acceptance.

☒ Drawee states that he has not yet obtained from our authorities the license that is necessary for payment/acceptance/withdraw of the goods.

☐ Drawee requests delivery of documents free of payment, since the payment has already been made directly to the drawer.

☐ Please refer to the attached copy of the drawee's/drawee's bank's letter under these circumstances, we shall hold the documents at your disposal pending receipt of your further instructions.

Canadian Imperial Bank of Commerce

3. 拒付电文一

Our Ref: FX REM 7795

Your Ref: 180CC 07135

Date: 16 Sept. 2001

Re: Your cheque sent for
collection dd 3 Sept. 2001
for HKD383 904.00

Referring to your above mentioned collection, subject cheque was returned unpaid for the reason of "STOP PAYMENT"

Please acknowledge receipt by signing and returning the duplicate of this letter to us.

For CHINA CONSTRUCTION BANK

4. 拒付电文二

Re: your Ref G-01-O-J-20686

Our Ref IBl80-920535

Drawer: Glory Profit Development Ltd

We regret to advise you that the drawee refused to pay the bills claiming the following reason:

The goods under the captioned item to be re-exported to Hong Kong but Beneficiary's reciprocal L/C not issued, Kindly give us your instructions for further disposal of documents so as to close our file.

For Midland Bank Ltd., London

5. 拒付电文三

Your Ref G-01-O-J-20686

Our Bill No. IB180-920535 Drawn by Haiyi Textile Imp. & Exp. Co.

As instructed in your telex, we enclose herewith the drafts and documents relating to the captioned collection for your withdrawal closing our records of this item.

As to our handling charges USDXXX being 0.125% commission on bill amount plus postage & cable charges USDXXX Please let us have your check or pay/credit to our account with quoting our Ref No.

Kindly acknowledge receipt by signing and returning to us the attached copy of this Letter.

For Bank of China, New York

拒付 问题	退票通知书一	退票通知书二	拒付电文一	拒付电文二	拒付电文三
拒付理由					
托收行的处理					

五、结果分析

1. 托收委托书（申请书）填写的完整性与准确性分析。
2. 托收指示缮制的正确性和明确性分析。
3. 跟单托收操作流程的准确性与高效性分析。

实验四

信用证结算业务

一、实验目的

1. 开证申请书填写完整、准确性的审核。
2. 根据开证申请书正确缮制信用证。
3. 掌握信用证的审证要求。
4. 信用证通知、保兑的处理。
5. 信用证修改的处理流程。
6. 信用证中议付、寄单索偿的处理。
7. 跟单信用证处理流程。
8. 掌握UCP600对信用证业务处理中的规定。

二、实验原理

（一）进口信用证业务知识点

1. 信用证业务的处理（Letter of Credit）

信用证是银行（开证行）根据买方（申请人）的要求和指示，向卖方（受益人）开立的，在一定期限内，凭符合信用证条款的单据，即期或在一个可以确定的将来日期，支付一定金额的书面承诺。国际贸易中最常见的跟单信用证基本程序见图4-1。

如图4-1所示，进口信用证业务（Import Letter of Credit）环节包括：

① 进、出口商签订合同，采用信用证结算方式；

② 进口商向银行提交开证申请书、保证金或其他担保品申请开立信用证；

③ 开证银行开立信用证，要求出口地银行通知或转递信用证；

⑩ 开证行审单无误后，向出口地银行偿付信用证下的金额，或由偿付行按信用证条款偿付；

⑪ 开证行通知进口商付款赎单；

⑫ 进口商付款后，开证行将单据交给进口商；

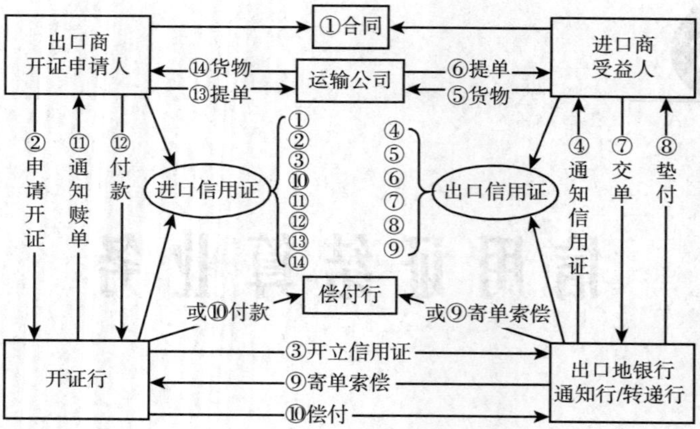

图 4－1　跟单信用证业务基本程序

⑬ 进口商向运输公司提交提单；

⑭ 进口商提取货物。

出口信用证业务（Export Letter of Credit）环节包括：

④ 通知行或转递行将信用证通知受益人或将信用证原件交受益人；

⑤～⑥ 受益人装船发货，取得提单，在此前后取得并缮制信用证要求的所有单据；

⑦ 受益人将单据提交给信用证中指定银行办理议付（付款或承兑）；

⑧ 出口地银行审单无误后，向受益人进行垫付；

⑨ 出口地银行向开证行寄单索汇，或向信用证中指定的偿付行索偿。

2. 信用证业务中的当事人

如图 4－2 所示，开证行以开证申请书为依据开立信用证，信用证业务中各方当事人受信用证约束，应按信用证规定办理通知、审证、审单、付款的业务处理。此外，信用证各方当事人还应严格遵循跟单信用证统一惯例（UCP600）的规定。

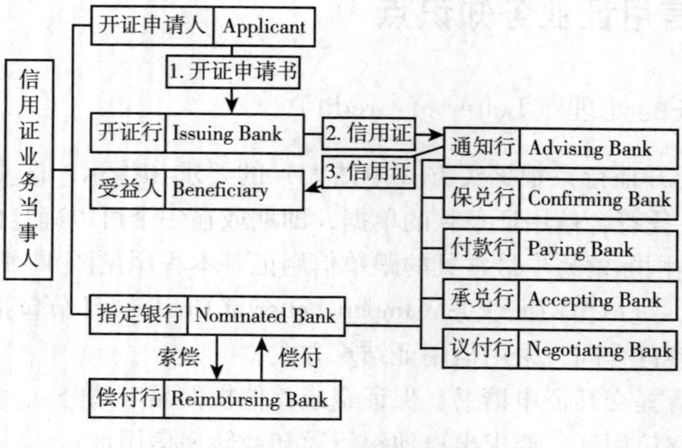

图 4－2　信用证业务当事人

3. 开证行业务处理环节和要求

开证行业务处理环节和要求见图 4－3。

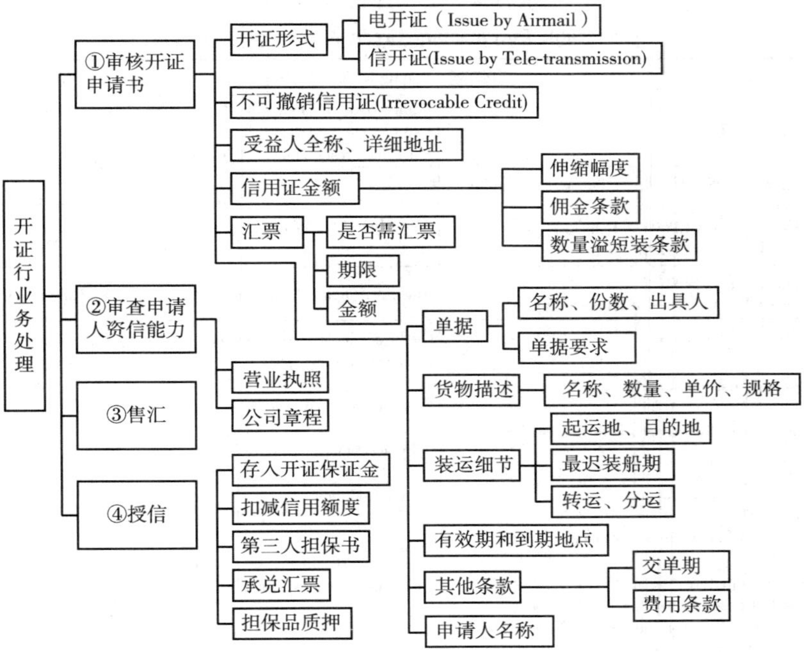

图 4 –3　开证行业务处理环节

4. 信用证的开立

（1）信用证的内容

实务中，信用证开立时并无统一格式，但各银行一般都会参照国际商会出版物 516 推荐的标准跟单信用证格式缮制信用证。开证申请书格式见示样 4 – 1。

（2）信用证开立的形式

开证行开立信用证可以通过电报、电传、SWIFT 或空邮传递至出口地通知行，一般国内开证都采用 SWIFT，电传基本已取消，但有时候境外银行开证仍采用电传开立。信用证开立的形式见图 4 –4。信开信用证格式见示样 4 –2 和示样 4 –3。实务中，SWIFT 开证主要采用 SWIFT700 格式，SWIFT700 开证格式见表 4 – 1。

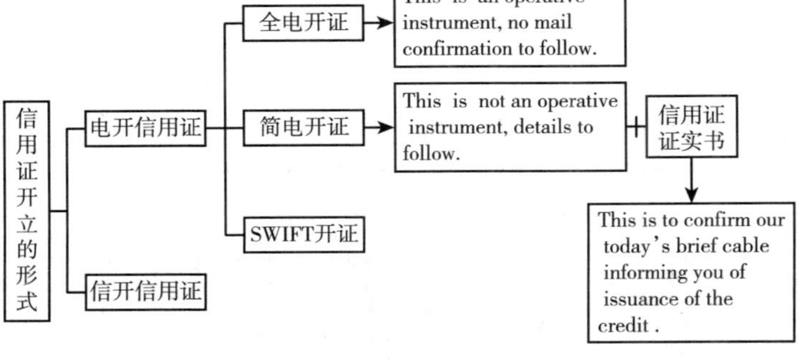

图 4 –4　信用证开立的形式

示样 4－1　开证申请书

Irrevocable Documentary Credit Application（正面）

<table>
<tr><td>Applicant：申请人</td><td>Issuing Bank：开证行</td></tr>
<tr><td>Date of Application：申请开证日期</td><td>Expiry Date and Place for Presentation of Documents
Expiry Date：到期日
Place for Presentation：到期地点</td></tr>
<tr><td rowspan="2">□Issue by（air）mail□with brief advice by teletransmission 开证形式（see UCP600 Article 11）
□Issue by teletransmission（see UCP600 Article 11）
□Transferable Credit－As per UCP600 Article 38</td><td></td></tr>
<tr><td>Beneficiary：受益人</td></tr>
<tr><td>Confirmation of the Credit 是否需保兑
□not requested □requested □authorised if requested by Beneficiary</td><td>Amount in figures and words（please use ISO Currency Codes）：金额</td></tr>
<tr><td>Partial shipments □allowed □not allowed
分运</td><td rowspan="4">Credit available with Nominated Bank：付款方式
□by payment at sight
□by deferred payment at：
□by acceptance of drafts at：
□by negotiation</td></tr>
<tr><td>Transshipments □allowed □not allowed
转运
Please refer to UCP600 Articles for exceptions to this condition</td></tr>
<tr><td>□Insurance will be covered by us
投保人</td></tr>
<tr><td rowspan="2">Shipment as defined in UCP600
Place of Taking in Charge/Dispatch from.../Place of Receipt：接管地/发货地/收货地
Port of Loading/Airport of Departure：装货港口/起飞航空港
Port of Discharge/Airport of destination：卸货港/目的地航空港
Place of Final Destination/For Transportation to.../Place of Delivery：货物发运最终目的地/转运至……/交货地
Not later than：最迟装船期</td></tr>
<tr><td>Against the documents detailed herein：汇票
□and Beneficiary's draft（s）drawn on：</td></tr>
<tr><td>Goods：
货物描述</td><td>Terms：价格条件
□FAS　□CIF
□FOB　□Other terms：
□CFR　□as per INCOTERMS</td></tr>
<tr><td colspan="2">单据要求
Commercial invoice □signed original□copies
Transport Documents：
□Multimode Transport Document，covering at least two different modes of transport
□Marine/Ocean Bill of Lading covering a port-to-port shipment
□Non-Negotiable Sea Waybill covering a port-to-port shipment
□Air Waybill，original for the consignor
□Other transport document
□to the order of
□endorsed in blank
□marked freight□prepaid□payable at destination
□notify：
Insurance Document：
□Policy□Certificate□Declaration under an open cover. Covering the following risks：
Certificates：
□Origin
□Analysis
□Health
□Other
Other Documents
□Packing List
□Weight List</td></tr>
<tr><td colspan="2">Documents to be presented within □ days after the date of shipment but within the validity of the credit.
交单期</td></tr>
<tr><td>Additional Instructions：
其他特别指示</td><td>We request you to issue on our behalf and for our account your Irrevocable Credit in accordance with the above instructions（marked（X）where appropriate）.
This credit will be subject to the Uniform Customs and Practice for Documentary Credits（2007 Revision，Publication No. 600 of the International Chamber of Commerce，Paris，France）insofar as they are applicable.
本证受 UCP600 约束

申请人签名
Signature of the Applicant</td></tr>
</table>

Secured Agreement for Letter of Credit（背面）

1. In consideration of your granting above request, we hereby guarantee that all drafts drawn and negotiated in compliance with terms and conditions of this credit shall be paid only at maturity.

2. Banks assume no liability or responsibility for the form, sufficiency, accuracy, genuineness, falsification or legal effect of any documents, or for the general and/or particular conditions stipulated in the documents or superimposed thereon.

3. We further agree that the title to all property which shall be purchased and/or shipped under this letter of credit, the documents relating thereto and the whole of the proceeds thereof, shall be and remain in your bank until the payment of the drafts or of all sums that may be due said drafts or otherwise and until the payment of any and all other indebtedness and liability, now existing or now or hereafter created or incurred by us to your bank due or not due, it being understood that the said documents and the merchandise represented thereby and all our other property, including securities and deposit balances, which may now or hereafter be in your bank or your branches possession otherwise subject to your control shall be deemed to be collateral security for the payment of the said drafts.

4. We hereby authorize you to dispose of the aforementioned property by public or private sale at your discretion without notice to us whenever we shall fail to accept or pay the said drafts on due date or whenever in your discretion, it is deemed necessary for the protection of yourselves and after deducting all your expenses to reimburse yourselves out of the proceeds.

5. And we further agree that you are not responsible for any errors or delays in transmission or interpretation of said letter of credit or for loss or late or non-arrival of part or of all the aforesaid documents, or the quality or value or the merchandise represented by same, or for any loss or damage which may happen to said merchandise whether during its transit by sea, after its arrival or by reason of the non-insurance or insufficient insurance thereof or by whatever cause or for the stoppage, or detention thereof by shipper or any party whomsoever, engaging ourselves duly to accept and pay such drafts in all like instances.

5. In case this request is signed by two or more, all promises or agreements made hereunder shall be joint and several, we herewith being ourselves to settle exchange on drafts drawn under this letter of credit with your good selves.

7. The applicant is also requested to observe the Uniform Customs and Practice for Documentary Credit fixed by the International Chamber of Commerce 2007 Revision Publication No. 600.

示样 4－2　信开信用证格式（受益人）

Advice for the Beneficiary

Name of Issuing Bank：开证行	Irrevocable Documentary Credit　　Number 不可撤销跟单信用证　　号码
Place and Date of Issue： 开证地点、日期	Expiry date and Place for Presentation of documents Expiry Date：到期日 Place for Presentation：到期地点
Applicant：申请人	
Advising Bank：　　Reference No. 通知行　　业务备查号	Beneficiary：受益人
	Amount：金额
Partial shipments □allowed 分运　□not allowed	Credit available with Nominated Bank：付款方式 □by payment at sight □by deferred payment at： □by acceptance of drafts at： □by negotiation
Transshipments □allowed 转运　□not allowed	
□Insurance will be covered by buyers 投保人	
Shipment as defined in UCP600 Place of Taking in Charge/Dispatch from.../Place of Receipt：接管地/发货地/收货地 Port of Loading/Airport of Departure：装货港口/起飞航空港 Port of Discharge/Airport of destination：卸货港/目的地航空港 Place of Final Destination/For Transportation to.../Place of Delivery：货物发运最终目的地/转运至……/交货地 Not later than：最迟装船期	Against the documents detailed herein：汇票 □and Beneficiary's draft（s）drawn on：
单据要求	
Documents to be presented within □ days after the date of shipment but within the validity of the credit. 交单期	
We hereby issue the Irrevocable Documentary Credit in your favor. It is subject to the Uniform Customs and Practice for Documentary Credit（2007 Revision，International Chamber of Commerce，Paris，France，Publication No. 600）and engages us in accordance with the terms thereof. The number and the date of the Credit and the name of our bank must be quoted on all drafts required. If the Credit is available by negotiable，each presentation must be noted on the reverse side of this advice by the bank where the Credit is available. 开证行保证付款条款；议付金额背批条款 开证行签名 Signature of the Issuing Bank This document consists of□ signed page（s）	

示样4－3 信开信用证格式（通知行）

Advice for the Advising Bank

Name of Issuing Bank：开证行

Irrevocable
Documentary Credit　　Number
不可撤销跟单信用证　　号码

Place and Date of Issue：
开证地点、日期

Expiry date and Place for Presentation of documents
Expiry Date：到期日
Place for Presentation：到期地点

Applicant：申请人

Advising Bank：　　Reference No.
通知行号　　业务备查 ↙

Beneficiary：受益人

Amount：金额

Partial shipments □allowed
分运　　□not allowed

Transshipments □allowed
转运　　□not allowed

□Insurance will be covered by buyers

Credit available with Nominated Bank：付款方式
□by payment at sight
□by deferred payment at：
□by acceptance of drafts at：
□by negotiation

Against the documents detailed herein：汇票
□and Beneficiary's draft（s） drawn on：

Shipment as defined in UCP600
Place of Taking in Charge/Dispatch from.../Place of Receipt：接管地/发货地/收货地
Port of Loading/Airport of Departure：装货港口/起飞航空港
Port of Discharge/Airport of destination：卸货港/目的地航空港
Place of Final Destination/For Transportation to.../Place of Delivery：货物发运最终目的地/转运至……/交货地
Not later than：最迟装船期

单据要求

Documents to be presented within □ days after the date of shipment but within the validity of the credit. 交单期

We hereby issue the Irrevocable Documentary Credit in your favor. It is subject to the Uniform Customs and Practice for Documentary Credit（2007 Revision，International Chamber of Commerce. Paris. France. Publication No. 600） and engages us in accordance with the terms thereof. We request you to advise the Beneficiary：
□without adding your confirmation　□adding your confirmation
□adding your confirmation，if requested by the beneficiary
Bank to Bank instruction：
开证行保证付款条款；保兑指示条款

开证行签名
Signature of the Issuing Bank

This document consists of□ signed page（s）

表 4 - 1　　　　　　　　　　**MT700 开证格式**

M/O	Tag	Field Name	
M	27	Sequence of total	报文页次
M	40A	Form of Credit	跟单信用证形式
M	20	Documentary Credit Number	跟单信用证号码
O	23	Reference to Pre-Advice	预先通知编码
O	31C	Date of issue	开证日期
M	40E	Applicable Rules	适用规则
M	31D	Date and place of expiry	最迟交单日期和交单地点
O	51a	Applicant Bank	开证申请人的银行
M	50	Applicant	开证申请人
M	59	Beneficiary	受益人
M	32B	Currency Code, Amount	货币和金额
O	39A	Percentage Credit Amount Tolerance	信用证金额上、下浮动最大允许范围
O	39B	Maximum Credit Amount	信用证金额最高限额
O	39C	Additional Amounts Covered	信用证涉及的附加金额
M	41a	Available with... by...	兑用银行及信用证兑用方式
O	42C	Drafts at...	汇票付款期限
O	42a	Drawee	汇票付款人
O	42M	Mixed Payment Details	混合付款细节
O	42P	Deferred Payment Details	迟期付款细节
O	43P	Partial Shipments	分批装运条款
O	43T	Transshipment	转运条款
O	44A	Place of Taking in Charge/Dispatch from.../Place of Receipt	接管地/发运地/收货地
O	44E	Port of Loading/Airport of Departure	装货港口/起飞航空港
O	44F	Port of Discharge/Airport of Destination	卸货港/目的地航空港
O	44B	Place of Final Destination/For Transportation to.../Place of Delivery	货物发运最终目的地/转运至……/交货地
O	44C	Latest Date of Shipment	最迟装运期
O	44D	Shipment Period	装运期
O	45A	Description of Goods and/or Services	货物/劳务描述
O	46A	Documents required	单据要求
O	47A	Additional Conditions	附加条款
O	71B	Charges	费用负担
O	48	Period for Presentation	交单期限
M	49	Confirmation Instructions	保兑指示
O	53a	Reimbursement Bank	偿付行
O	78	Instructions to the Paying/Accepting/Negotiating Bank	给付款行，承兑行或议付行的指示
O	57a	"Advise Through" bank	通知行
O	72	Sender to Receiver Information	附言

表 4 - 1 内部分项目填写要求如下：

27：报文页次。如果跟单信用证条款能够全部容纳在 MT700 报文中，那么该项目内应填入“1/1”。如果跟单信用证内容超过 MT700 报文格式的容量时，可以使用一个或几个（最多三个）MT701 报文格式传送有关跟单信用证条款。此时，在 MT700 中填入“1/2”，在 MT701 中填入“2/2”，依此类推。

40A：跟单信用证形式。该项目共有三种填法，“IRREVOCABLE”为不可撤销跟单信用证；“IRREVOCABLE TRANSFERABLE”为不可撤销可转让跟单信用证；“IRREVOCABLE STANDBY”为不可撤销备用信用证。

23：预先通知编码。如果采用此格式开立的信用证已被预先通知，此项目内应填入“PREADV/”，后跟预先通知的编号或日期。

40E：适用规则。包括以下几种表示：“UCP LATEST VERSION”，即“跟单信用证遵循现时有效的巴黎国际商会制定的《跟单信用证统一惯例》，并于开证日生效”；“EUCP LATEST VERSION”，即“跟单信用证遵循现时有效的巴黎国际商会制定的《跟单信用证统一惯例电子交单规则》，并于开证日生效”；“UCPURR LATEST VERSION”，即“跟单信用证遵循现时有效的巴黎国际商会制定的《跟单信用证统一惯例》和《银行间偿付统一规则》，并于开证日生效”；“EUCPURR LATEST VERSION”，即“跟单信用证遵循现时有效的巴黎国际商会制定的《跟单信用证统一惯例电子交单规则》和《银行间偿付统一规则》，并于开证日生效”；“ISP LATEST VERSION”，即“备用信用证遵循现时有效的巴黎国际商会制定的《国际备用证管理》，并于开证日生效”。

51a：开证申请人的银行。如果开证行和开证申请人的银行不是同一家银行，则使用该项目列明开证申请人的银行。

39A：信用证金额浮动允许范围。该项目列明信用证金额上、下浮动的最大允许范围，用百分比表示，如“10/10”表示允许上、下浮动各不超过 10%。

39B：信用证金额最高限额。该项目填写“UP TO”，“MAXIMUM”或“NOT EXCEEDING”（后跟金额），表示跟单信用证金额的最高限额。此项目不能与 39A 同时出现。

39C：附加金额。该项目列明信用证所涉及的附加金额，如保险费、运费、利息等。

41a：有关银行及信用证兑付方式。①银行的表示：当项目代号为“41A”时，银行用 SWIFT 名址码表示；当项目代号为“41D”时，银行用行名地址表示。如果信用证为自由议付信用证时，该项目代号应为“41D”，银行用“ANY BANK IN...”表示；如果该信用证为自由议付信用证，而且对议付地点也无限制时，该项目代号应为“41D”，银行用“ANY BANK”表示。②兑付方式的表示：“BY PAYMENT”为即期付款；“BY ACCEPTANCE”为远期承兑；“BY NEGOTIATION”为议付；“BY DEF PAYMENT”为延期付款；“BY MIXED PAYMENT”为混合付款。

42a：汇票付款人。该项目列明跟单信用证下汇票的付款人，必须与 42C 汇票付款期限同时出现。该项目内不能出现账号。

44A：接管地、发运地、接受地。该项目列明货物接管地点（在使用多式联运提单时），接受地（公路、铁路、内陆水运单据、信件、快递服务单据），标注货运单据上的发运地。

44C：最迟装运日期。该项目列明对最迟装船、发运和接受监管的日期，不能与 44D 装运期同时出现。

71B：费用负担。该项目的出现只表示费用由受益人负担。若报文无此项目，则表示除议付费、转让费外，其他费用均由开证申请人负担。

48：交单期限。该项目列明在开立运输单据后多少天内交单。若报文未使用该项目，则表示在开立运输单据后 21 天内交单。

49：保兑指示。当该项目为“CONFIRM”时，要求收报行保兑该信用证；当该项目为“MAY ADD”，表示收报行可以对信用证加保兑；当该项目为“WITHOUT”，表示不要求收报行保兑该信用证。

72：附言。当该项目为“/PHONBEN/”时，表示用电话通知受益人；当该项目为“/TELEBEN/”时，表示用快捷有效的电讯方式通知受益人。

5. 开证行审单后的处理

开证行收到被指定行，亦称索偿行（Claiming Bank）或寄单行寄来的单据后，应合理谨慎地审核单据，缮制进口单到通知书或进口押汇通知书通知申请人。开证行审单处理基本程序见图 4－5。

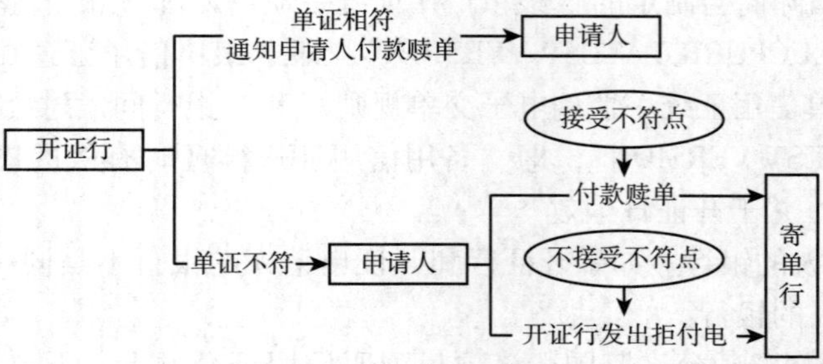

图 4－5　开证行审单处理基本程序

开证行审单相符付款后，一般都根据索偿行的要求，以邮寄或电讯方式发出付款通知书。付款通知书格式见示样 4－4。

示样 4－4　付款通知书

Your Ref. No. BP－05205 dated 24/11/93

Our Ref. IBB41572

Drawn under our L/C No. CBB43306

Draft for HKD456, 000. 00

In settlement of the above mentioned drawing, we have today remitted the net proceeds to you via CHATS as instructed, you may release indemnity/lift the reserves, if any.

Draft Amt HKD 456, 000. 00	Less our charges:
[X] Cable charges 200. 00	☐ Commission in lieu of exchange
[X] Discrepancy fee 200. 00	☐ CHATS Charges

Net proceeds HKD 455 600. 00

若开证行审单不符拒付，应向寄单行发出拒付通知书，拒付通知书格式见示样 4－5 和 4－6。

示样 4 –5　拒付通知书

Please quote this No.

in all correspondence　　　　　　　　　Our Ref. No.　　Date:

To:

Dear sir,

Re: Your Bill Ref. ______________________

for ______________________

under our L/C No. ______________________

We have to advise you that upon checking the above captioned documents the following discrepancy (ies) has/have been found:

...

In view of these discrepancies, please note the following paragraphs marked (X):

☐Payment/Acceptance has been refused.

☐We return to you herewith the above documents.

☐We now hold the documents at your disposal and wait your instructions.

☐Please refund us through ______________ under advice to us, the amount of ______________ already claimed by you.

☐Payment/Acceptance of the above documents is considered to have made UNDER RESERVE. We shall advise you as soon as the reserve can be lifted.

☐Please obtain and forward to us amended ______________ in order to enable us to re-consider the payment/acceptance of the documents.

示样 4 –6　拒付通知书

RE: YR REF BP18141041 FOR USD60 800. – (拒付信用证概况)

OUR REF IBP00314 UNDER ILC00149

UPON CHECKING THE ABOVE DOCUMENTS, WE FOUND THE FOLLOWING DISCREPANCIES AS BELOWS: (拒付原因)

1. LATE NEGOTIATION.

2. ON BOARD NOTATION WITHOUT SIGNATURE.

3. PHOTOCOPY OF QTY INSPECTION PRESENTED I/O ORIGINAL AND NOT AUTHENTICATED.

4. INV. OF N32 –91CL SHOWING TYPING ERROR:

1. 25 AT USD2 450. 00 = USD18 424. 00

5. RABBIT-L-GRADE OVERSHIPPED, RABBIT-M-GRADE SHORTSHIPED.

WE ARE WAITING THE APPLICANT'S ACCEPTANCE AND SHALL REVERT.

DOCUMENTS AT YOUR DISPOSAL INSTRUCTION. (拒付后的处理)

(二) 出口信用证业务知识点

出口地银行业务处理环节和要求见图 4 –6。

如图 4 –6 所示，出口地银行收到开证行发送的信用证后，要经过通知、修改、保兑、审单付款/议付和寄单索偿等环节的处理。其中，信用证修改基本程序见图 4 –7，信用证常见修改条款见表 4 –2，MT707 跟单信用证的修改电文格式见表 4 –3。

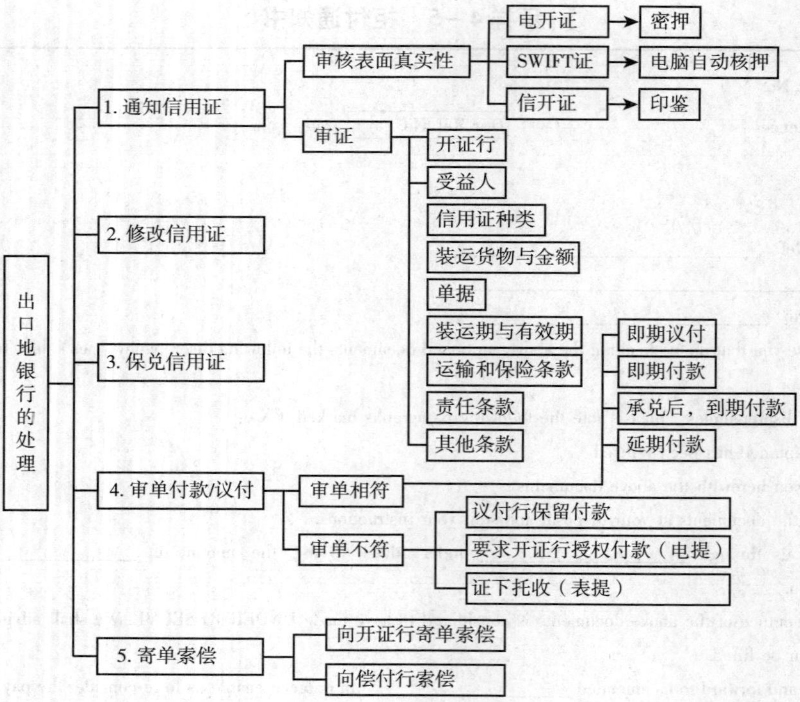

图4－6　出口地银行处理环节

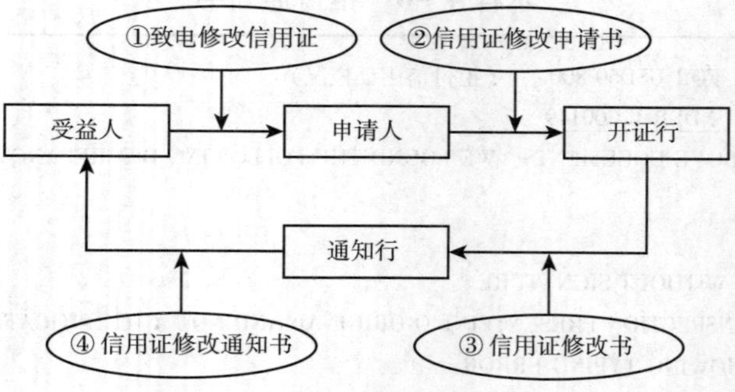

图4－7　信用证修改基本程序

表4－2　　　　　　信用证常见修改条款

1	装运日期和有效期的展延	Latest shipment and expiry date extend to ________ and ________ respectively.
2	金额和货物数量的增减	L/C increased (decreased) by 原信用证金额 to 修改后金额 and quantity of commodities increased (decreased) by 原数量 to 修改后数量.
3	保险险别的改变	Insurance covering all risks instead of F. P. A.
4	装运港、目的港的更改	Shipment from 修改后装运港 to 修改后目的港 instead of previously stipulated. /Port of destination amended to read 修改后目的港 instead of 原目的港.
5	提单抬头人修改	B/L made out to order of 修改后抬头人 instead of previously stipulated.
6	允许分批装运	Partial shipments permitted.

7	允许转运，或允许在某地转运	Transshipment permitted/Transshipment at HongKong permitted.
8	单价改变	Unit price now changed to read 修改后单价 instead of 原单价.
9	贸易条件修改	Trade terms amended to be on CIF New York（修改后贸易条件）instead of FOB Shanghai（原贸易条件）.
10	运保费改由另一方负担	Freight and insurance premium to be paid by beneficiary/applicant.
11	一切银行费用由申请人承担	All banking charges are for applicant account.
12	删除某条款和插入某新条款	Delete the clause："________". Insert a new clause："________".
13	请通知行加保兑	Please add your confirmation to this credit，your confirmation charges，if any，are for applicant/beneficiary account.

表 4－3　　MT707 跟单信用证修改格式

M/O	Tag	Field Name	
M	20	Sender's Reference	发报行的编号
M	21	Receiver's Reference	收报行的编号
O	23	Issuing Bank's Reference	开证行的编号
O	52a	Issuing Bank	开证行
O	31c	Date of Issue	开证日期
O	30	Date of Amendment	修改日期
O	26E	Number of Amendment	修改次数
M	59	Beneficiary（before this amendment）	受益人
O	31E	New Date of Expiry	修改后的到期日
O	32B	Increase of Documentary Credit Amount	跟单信用证的增额
O	33B	Decrease of Documentary Credit Amount	跟单信用证的减额
O	34B	New Documentary Credit Amount after Amendment	修改后的信用证金额
O	39A	Percentage Credit Amount Tolerance	修改后的信用证金额浮动上下限
O	39B	Maximum Credit Amount	修改后的信用证金额最高限额
O	39C	Additional Amounts Covered	附加金额
O	44A	Place of Taking in Charge/Dispatch from.../ Place of Receipt	对接管地、发运地、收货地的修改
O	44E	Port of Loading/Airport of Departure	对装货港口/起飞航空港的修改
O	44F	Port of Discharge/Airport of Destination	对卸货港口/目的地航空港的修改
O	44B	Place of Final Destination/For Transportation to.../Place of Delivery	对最终目的地/运往……/交货地点的修改
O	44C	Latest Date of Shipment	对最迟装运期的修改
O	44D	Shipment Period	对装运期的修改
O	79	Narrative	修改详述
O	72	Sender to Receiver Information	附言

出口地银行（寄单行）审单相符后，应按信用证的索偿指示向开证行或偿付行索偿。寄单行向开证行进行索偿的基本程序见图4－8，寄单行向偿付行索偿的基本程序见图4－9。

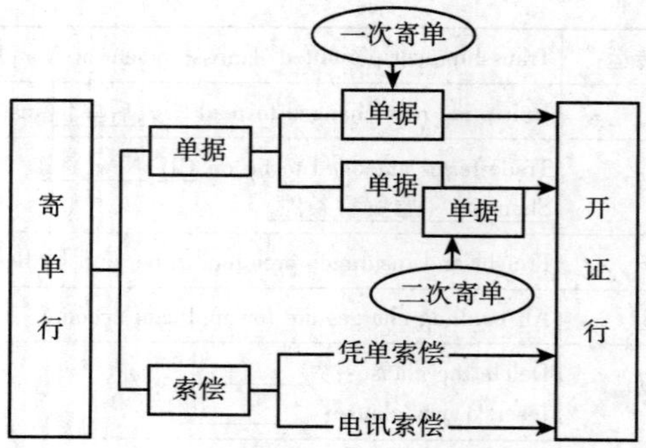

图 4-8　寄单行向开证行索偿基本程序

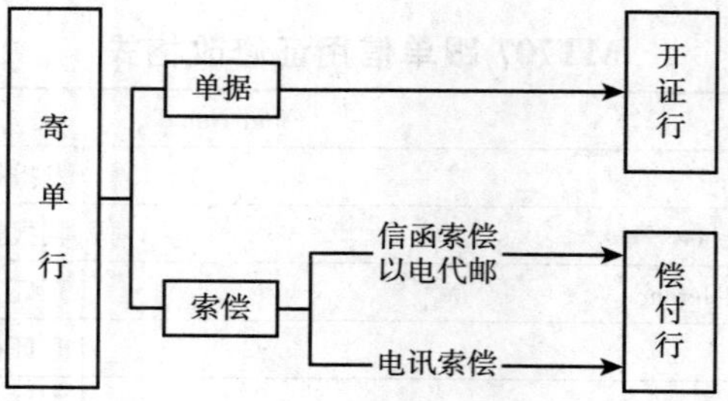

图 4-9　寄单行向偿付行索偿基本程序

三、实验内容

1. 开证行审核开证申请书。
2. 开证行缮制全电证、简电证、SWIFT 格式信用证。
3. 通知行审核信用证、通知信用证。
4. 开证行、通知行处理信用证的修改。
5. 出口地银行议付、付款的处理。
6. 寄单行寄单索偿的处理。
7. 开证行通知进口商单到付款的处理。

四、实验步骤

（一）开证申请书的审核

2003 年 5 月 10 日，CHINA IMP. & EXP. CORP. GUANGDONG 向中国银行广东省分行提交下面这张开证申请书申请开证，开证行按所给问题审核开证申请书。

APPLICATION FOR IRREVOCABLE DOCUMENTARY CREDIT

致：中国银行广东省分行 | LC NO. 230BS－453222 |

TO：BANK OF CHINA，GUANGDONG BRANCH

日期：

DATE：MAY 10，2003

兹请贵行以□信开 X 电开按下述项目开立不可撤销信用证 Please issue by ~~airmail~~/cable an irrevocable letter of credit as follows	有效期 Expiry Date：July 30，2003 在受益人所在国 In the beneficiary's country
申请人 APPLICANT（Name & Address） CHINA IMP. & EXP. CORP. GUANGDONG INTERNATIONAL BUILDING，DONGFENGXI RD.， GUANGZHOU，P. R. CHINA TEL：89676777	受益人 Beneficiary（Name & Address） PHILIPS HONG KONG LIMITED CS/BUSINESS COMMUNICATION SYSTEM 26/F，HOPEWELL CENTRE，17 KENNEDY RD. HONG KONG TEL：8215888/8215688
通知行（如未填写贵行可自选）ADVISING BANK（IF BLANK，AT YOUR OPTION）	金额 Amount（in figures and words） USD77，495.79 SAY U. S. DOLLARS SEVENTY SEVEN THOUSAND FOUR HUNDRED NINETY FIVE AND CENTS SEVENTY NINE ONLY

本证使用时，汇票由你行选定以本公司或你行代理行为付款人见票　天，贵行按　%的发票金额支用，随附下列单据。
Available by draft drawn，at your option，on us/you or your correspondent at sight for 100% of the invoice value accompanied by the following documents.

X 商业发票一式　份标明信用证号码和合同号码。
Signed commercial invoice in copies indicating L/C No. and Contract No..

□全套清洁已装船海运提单/铁路运输承运货物收据作成空白抬头由发货人空白背书注明“运费付讫/运费待收”并通知________
Full set of clean on board OCEAN BILLS OF LADING /FORWARDING AGENT'S RAILWAY CARGO RECEIPTS made out to order and endorsed in blank，marked FREIGHT PREPAID/FREIGHT TO COLLECT and notify ____________

X 洁净航空提单以贵行为收货人注明“运费付讫/运费待收”及列明信用证号码并通知开证申请人。
Clean Air Waybill consigned to your bank marked Freight Collect showing this L/C No. and notify the applicant with full address.

□保险单或保险凭证一式　份空白背书按　%的 CIF 金额注明赔款在目的地以汇票同种货币支付投保：学会货物险条款（一切险/平安险）、学会战争险、学会罢工暴动民变险。
Insurance policy/certificate in copies blank endorsed，for pct of the CIF value showing claims payable at destination in the same currency as the draft and covering：Institute Cargo Clauses（A/B/C），Institute War Clauses and Institute S. R. C. C. Clauses.

X 装箱单或重量单　份 Packing list/weight memo in 4 copies

X 由　出具之品质证　份 Certificate of quality in 4 copies issued by the manufacturers.

X 由　出具之产地证　份 Certificate of origin in 3 copies issued by the Chamber of Commerce in the country of Origin.

X Beneficiary's copy of cable to the accountecs advising shipment immediately after shipment made.

装运货物 Covering shipment of：COMPONENTS FOR SOPHO－S 451482－155200 SHIPPING MARKS＝03EMHKHNCT02002
QUANTITY：1 LOT　FCA AMSTERDAM　GUANGZHOU CHINA

由 shipment from AMSTERDAM 装运至 To GUANGZHOU 不迟于 Latest：July 15，2003	分批装运 Partial Shipments X 准许 allowed □禁止 prohibited	转运 Transshipment X 准许 allowed □禁止 prohibited

其他条款：（下列条款遇有与上列印妥条款有明显出入时，则以下列条款为准）。
OTHER TERMS AND CONDITIONS（These shall prevail over all printed terms in case of any apparent conflict）
中国广州以外的一切银行费用由受益人负担。All banking charges outside Guangzhou，China are for beneficiary's account.
单据须在装运单据签发日之后　天内但不超过信用证有效期内提交。
Documents must be presented within 15 days after the date of issuance of the shipping document（s）but within the validity of the credit.

开证申请人签章
Stamp & Signature of Applicant

本表用英文填写。第一联银行留存（本证受国际商会现行“统一惯例”制约 Subject to UCP ICC prevailing revision）

(1) 申请人公司	
(2) 受益人公司	
(3) 通知行是否已由申请人指定?	
(4) 信用证到期地点和时间	
(5) 受益人开立汇票的要求	
(6) 单据种类、份数、要求	
(7) 货物装运港、目的港、最迟装船期	
(8) 能否分运? 能否转运?	
(9) 银行费用由哪方支付?	
(10) 交单期	
(11) 开证行处理信用证业务的依据是什么?	
(12) 开证行除审查申请书外,还应处理哪些事宜?	
(13) 开证行在什么情况下可免责?	

(二) 信用证的开立

中国银行广东省分行接受 CHINA IMP. & EXP. CORP. GUANGDONG 开证申请,于次日采用 SWIFT 对外开立信用证。

: 40A form of documentary credit:
: 20 documentary credit number:
: 31C date of issue:
: 31D date and place of expiry:
: 51s applicant bank:

: 50 applicant:

: 59 beneficiary:

: 32B currency code amount:
: 39A pct credit amount tolerance:
: 41A available with /by - swift addr:
: 42 drafts at drawn on:

: 43P partial shipments:
: 43T transshipment:
: 44A on board/disp/taking charge:
: 44B for transportation to:
: 44C latest date of shipment:

: 45A shipment of goods and/or services:
: 46A documents required:

: 47A additional conditions:

: 48 period for presentation

: 49 confirmation instruction:

53A reimbursement bank - BIC:

: 78 instructions to pay/acc/neg bk:

（三）信用证的审证

审核下面的信用证，对其存在的问题进行分析，并提出修改的意见。

: To: 1450 14BKCHCNBJA94099065
: FM: 1550 14MTRBJPJTAXXX0694
MTRBJPJTXXX
+ MITSUI TRUST AND BANKING CO.
+ LTD. THE
+ TOKYO
: MT: 700 01
: 40A form of documentary credit: IRREVOCABLE
: 20 documentary credit number: 100934028D - 01001
: 31C date of issue: 20090314
: 31D date and place of expiry: 20090515 P. R. OF CHINA
: 50 applicant: SUMITOMO CORPORATION,
2 - 2 HITOTSUBASHI, CHIYODA - KU
TOKYO
: 59 beneficiary: JIANGSU NATIVE PRODUCE IMF. AND EXP. (GROUP) CORP.
36 GONG YUAN ROAD. NANJING
THE PEOPLE'S REPUBLIC OF CHINA
: 32B amount: CURRENCY JP ￥3 078 075. 00
: 41 - : available with /by: ANY BANK BY NEGOTIATION
: 42C: drafts at... : DRAFT AT 180 DAYS DATE
: 42 - : drawee: THE MITSUI TRUST AND BANKING CO. LTD.
HEAD OFFICE, TOKYO
: 43p partial shipments: PROHIBITED
: 43T transshipment: PROHIBITED
: 44A loading in charge: CHINESE AIRPORT

: 44B for transportation to: NARITA, AIRPORT
: 44C latest date of shipment: 20090510
: 45A shipment of goods:

600 KGS NET OF CHINESE ROYAL JELLY (PRODUCTS
BY LAOSHAN FACTORY) IN REFRIGERATED CONTAINER
AT JP ¥4 510.00 PER KG NET. LESS DISC. 2.5%
CIF NARITA AIRPORT

: 46A: documents required:

+SIGNED COMMERCIAL INVOICE IN QUINTUPLICATE (5) INDICATING APPLICANT'S REF NO. MCC1-94-0120 WHICH MUST BE GIVEN ON ALL OTHER DOCUMENTS

+PACKING LIST IN DUPLICATE

+FULL SET OF CLEAN AIR WAYBILL CONSIGNED TO SUMITOMO CORPORATION TOKYO AND MARKED FREIGHT PREPAID AND SHOWING SAME NAMES AS NOTIFY PARTY AS CONSIGNEE AND INDICATING ACTUAL FLIGHT DATE

+FULL SET OF INSURANCE POLICIES OR CERTIFICATES ENDORSED IN BLANK, FOR 110PCT INVOICE VALUE COVERING THE INSTITUTE CARGO CLAUSES (ALL RISKS), AND THE INSTITUTE WAR CLAUSES AND THE INSTITUTE STRIKES RIOTS AND CIVIL COMMOTIONS CLAUSE AND I. O. P.
CLAIMS ARE PAYABLE IN JAPAN IN CURRENCY OF DRAFTS.
INSURANCE TO BE EFFECTED BY SHIPPER

+ORIGINAL GSP FORM A, CERTIFICATE OF NO ANTIBIOTICS AND COPIES OF CERTIFICATE OF QUALITY ALSO REQUIRED

: 47A: additional cond.:

1) SHIPPING MARKS SHOULD INCLUDE SUMIT IN TRIANGLE.
2) TRANSPORT DOCUMENTS WHICH BEAR REFERENCE BY STAMP OF OTHERWISE TO COSTS ADDITIONAL TO THE FREIGHT ARE NOT ACCEPTABLE.
3) ORIGINAL CERTIFICATE OF QUALITY CERTIFYING PRODUCTS BY LAOSHAN FACTORY, MOISTURE MAX 67.0PCT AND DECENOIC ACID MIN 2.1PCT ISSUED BY C. C. I. B. SHOULD BE ATTACHED TO THE CARGO AND A BENEFICIARIES' CERTIFICATE REQUIRED
4) DRAFT (S) TO ENFACE SAME DATE AS AIR WAYBILL AND WILL BE PAYABLE AT A FIXED DATE
5) The certificates of inspection would be issued and signed by authorized the applicant of L/C before shipment of cargo, which the signature will be inspected by issuing bank.

: 71B: details of charges: ALL BANKING CHARGES ARE FOR ACCOUNT OF APPLICANT.
: 48: presentation period: DRAFTS/DOCUMENTS MUST BE PRESENTED WITHIN 15 DAYS AFTER DATE OF ISSUANCE OF TRANSPORT DOCUMENTS, BUT WITHIN THE VALIDITY OF CREDIT
: 49 confirmation instruction: WITHOUT
: 53 - reimbursement bank: THE MITSUI TRUST AND BANKING CO., LTD., HEAD OFFICE, TOKYO
: 78 instructions:

THE NEGOTIATING BANK MUST FORWARD TO US (INT'L OPERATIONS ADMINISTRATION DIV. 1-1 NIHONBASHI MUROMACHI 2-CHOME. CHUO-KU TOKYO) ALL DOCUMENTS IN ONE REGISTERED AIRMAIL AND TO THE DRAWEE BANK THE DRAFTS TOGETHER WITH COMPLICANCE CERTIFICATE.
ALL DRAFTS DRAWN HERE UNDER MUST INDICATE NUMBER, DATE AND NAME OF ISSUING BANK OF THIS CREDIT.

-MAC/A1EB3306

（四）信用证的通知

1. 2002 年 3 月 24 日中国银行广州分行根据收到的信用证缮制信用证通知书，未加保兑。

<table>
<tr><td>Name of Issuing Bank:
BANK OF CHINA NEW YORK BRANCH</td><td rowspan="2">IRREVOCABLE DOCUMENTARY CREDIT
No. A－01－I－70498
ORIGINAL</td></tr>
<tr><td>Place and Date of Issue:
19 March, 2002, New York</td></tr>
<tr><td>Applicant
FILTHAI IMPORT CORP. LTD., NEW YORK
FLAT H, 16/F YOTHIN COURT, 118－128</td><td>Expiry date and Place for Presentation of documents
Expiry Date: 20 June, 2002
Place for Presentation: CHINA</td></tr>
<tr><td>Advising Bank
BANK OF CHINA
GUANGZHOU BRANCH</td><td>Beneficiary
GUANGZHOU FEI YUE SEWING MACHINE MANUFACTORY, 187 TIAN YUAN ROAD, GUANGZHOU, CHINA</td></tr>
<tr><td>Partial Shipment □Allowed [X] Not allowed

Transshipment □Allowed [X] Not allowed</td><td>Amount USD21 000.00
(SAY UNITED STATES DOLLARS TWENTY ONE THOUSAND ONLY)</td></tr>
<tr><td>Shipment from GUANGZHOU

to NEW YORK

Latest 31 May, 2002</td><td>Credit available with ANY BANK
□by payment at sight
□by deferred payment at:
□by acceptance of drafts at:
[X] by negotiation
against the documents detailed herein
[X] and of your drafts at sight for FULL invoice value drawn on us.</td></tr>
<tr><td colspan="2">[X] SIGNED COMMERCIAL INVOICE IN QUADRUPLICATE
[X] FULL SET OF CLEAN "ON BOARD" OCEAN BILLS OF LADING PLUS 2 NON-NEGOTIABLE COPIES MADE OUT TO ORDER AND ENDORSED IN BLANK MARKED "FREIGHT PREPAID" AND NOTIFY FILTHAI IMPORT CORP. LTD., NEW YORK WITH FULL ADDRESS
[X] INSURANCE POLICY (IES) OR CERTIFICATE (S) IN ASSIGNABLE FORM AND ENDORSED IN BLANK FOR 110 PCT CIF VALUE SHOWING CLAIMS PAYABLE AT NEW YORK IN THE SAME CURRENCY OF DRAFT, COVERING INSTITUTE CARGO CLAUSES (A), INSTITUTE WAR CLAUSES INCLUDING S. R. C. C. (IF SHIPMENT EFFECTED BY CONTAINERIZED VESSEL, INSURANCE ALSO TO COVER J. W. O. B. CLAUSES)
[X] PACKING LIST IN QUADRUPLICATE
[X] BENEFICIARY'S CERTIFICATE CERTIFYING THAT THEY HAVE SENT ONE SET OF NON－NEGOTIABLE SHIPPING DOCUMENTS DIRECTLY TO FILTHAI IMPORT CORP. LTD., NEW YORK BY AIRMAIL WITHIN 3 DAYS AFTER SHIPMENT
Covering shipment of:
SW-Ⅱ X 8 in wooden cases as per S/C No. HR34987 CIF NEW YORK SHIPPING MARKS = 02NGS/02602TH
GUANGZHOU CHINA</td></tr>
<tr><td colspan="2">Documents to be presented within [20] days after the date of shipment but within the validity of the credit.</td></tr>
<tr><td>We hereby issue the Irrevocable Documentary Credit in your favor. It is subject to the Uniform Customs and Practice for Documentary Credit (2007 Revision, International Chamber of Commerce, Paris, France, and Publication No. 600) and engages us in accordance with the terms thereof.
Yours faithfully
FOR BANK OF CHINA NEW YORK BRANCH
____
Authorized Signature (s)</td><td>1. If the credit is available by negotiation, each presentation must be noted on the reverse side of this advice by the bank where the credit is available.
2. All documents are to be dispatched in ONE lot by registered airmail to us.
3. The number and the date of the credit and the name of our bank must be quoted on all draft required.
4. In reimbursement of your payment made under this LC, we shall credit your account with us under our telex advice to you.</td></tr>
</table>

中国银行　广州分行

BANK OF CHINA GUANGZHOU BRANCH

ADDRESS：

信用证通知书

CABLE：

TELEX：

SWIFT：

FAX：

YEAR-MONTH-DATE

To：致：	WHEN CORRESPONDING PLEASE QUOTE OUR REF NO. 06001953
Issuing Bank 开证行	Transmitted to us through 转递行
L/C No. 信用证号 Dated 开证日期	Amount

Dear sirs，敬启者： ＊ SUBJECT TO UCP600

We have pleasure in advising you that we have received from the above bank a(n)

兹通知贵公司，我行收自上述银行

□Telex issuing 电传开立 □Ineffective 未生效

□Pre-advising of 预先通知 □Mail confirmation of 邮寄证实书

□Original 正本 □Duplicate 副本

Letter of credit，contents of which are as per attached sheet(s).

This advice and the attached sheet(s) must accompany the relative documents when presented for negotiation.

信用证一份，现随附通知。贵公司交单时，请将通知书及信用证一并提交。

□Please note that this advice does not constitute our confirmation at the above L/C nor does it convey any engagement or obligation on our party.

本通知书不构成我行对此信用证之保兑及其他任何责任。

□Please note that we have added our confirmation to the above L/C，negotiation is restricted to ourselves only.

上述信用证已由我行加具保兑，并限向我行交单。

Remarks：备注：

A. . . T/T Claim　　B.

C.　　D.

This L/C consists of 2 sheet (s)，including the covering letter and attachment(s).

本信用证连同面函及附件共　页。

If you find any terms and conditions in the L/C which you are unable to comply with and or any error(s)，it is suggested that you contact applicant directly for necessary amendment(s) so as.

如本信用证中有无法办到的条款或错误，请与开证申请人联系进行必要的修改，以排除交单时可能发生的问题。

As requested by our correspondent，we hereby confirm the abovementioned credit.

根据通汇银行要求，本银行确认本信用证。

Yours faithfully

For BANK OF CHINA
GUANGZHOU BRANCH

2. 受益人收到中国银行广州分行通知的信用证后，填写信用证分析单。

信用证分析单

银行编号		合约		受益人			
证　　号							
开证银行				进口商			
开证日期		索汇方式		起运口岸		目的地	
金　　额				可否转运			唛头
汇票付款人				可否分运			
汇票期限				装运期限			
注意事项				效期地点			
				提单日__天内议付	__天内寄单		

单证名称	提单	副提单	商业发票	VISA商业发票	海关发票	装箱单	重量单	尺码单	保险单	产地证	GSP产地证	EEC产地证	贸促会产地证	出口许可证	装船证书	投保通知	寄投保通知邮据	寄单证明	寄单邮据	铁路货物收据	电传副本	声明	
银行																							
客户																							

提单	抬头		保险				
	通知			保额另加　%	赔款地点		
运费预付							

This Documentary Credit is subject to the Uniform Customs and Practice.

如分析单内容与合约有不符或疑问，请查核信用证原本

分析单编号：

（五）信用证的修改

1. 受益人 GUANGZHOU FEI YUE SEWING MACHINE MANUFACTORY 审证后于 3 月 26 日向申请人 FILTHAI IMPORT CORP. LTD.，NEW YORK 发送信用证修改函电，3 月 28 日申请人据此向开证行提交信用证修改申请书，3 月 29 日开证行据此缮制信用证修改书电报发送至通知行。

信用证修改函电

TO: FILTHAI IMPORT CORP. LTD., NEW YORK
FM: GUANGZHOU FEI YUE SEWING MACHINE MANUFACTORY
DD 020326
Dear Sirs:

We have today received LC No. A－01－I－70498 covering the shipment of SW－Ⅱ X 8 in wooden cases as per S/C No. HR34987 CIF NEW YORK. After we have checked the LC carefully, we request you to make the following amendments:

1. The goods should read as: SW-Ⅱ X 6 in wooden cases.
2. LC amount should read: USD20 000.00
3. The latest shipment date to be extended to10 June and the validity of the credit to 30 June.
4. One copy original Bill of Lading should airmail to applicant immediately after shipment should be deleted.

Please confirm the amendments by telex, so that we may arrange shipment accordingly.

Yours faithfully

信用证修改申请书

To: Issuing Bank	**APPLICATION FOR AMENDMENT TO CREDIT**
Original stipulated in the credit	
Credit No.	Date of amendment
Name of advising bank	Place of amendment
Beneficiary	Amendment No. A－01－I－70498－786
Amount (Say)	Please amend following by Airmail Cable
Date of expiry	

This amendment is to be considered as part of the above mentioned credit and must be attached thereto.

Item	**Originals stipulated**	**Alteration to be made**

Remark: All other terms and conditions remain unchanged.

The above mentioned credit is subject to the Uniform Customs and Practice for Documentary Credits Revision 1993, ICC Publication 500.

Signature of Applicant

信用证修改书

<table>
<tr><td>To Advising Bank</td><td>AMENDMENT
TO DOCUMENTARY CREDIT
Number
Place and Date of Amendment</td></tr>
<tr><td>Applicant</td><td>Beneficiary</td></tr>
<tr><td>Issuing Bank

Ref. No.</td><td>This amendment is to be considered as part of the above mentioned credit.</td></tr>
<tr><td colspan="2">The above mentioned credit amended as follows:
____
____
____
____
____
____
____
____
____
____
All other terms and conditions remain unchanged.</td></tr>
<tr><td colspan="2">The above mentioned documentary credit is subject to the Uniform Customs and Practice for Documentary Credits 1993 Revision, ICC Publication No. 500.</td></tr>
<tr><td>Please advise the Beneficiary
Name and Signature of Issuing Bank
____
Address ____________________</td><td>Advising Bank's Notification
Name and Signature of Advising Bank
____
Address ____________________</td></tr>
</table>

2. 中国银行广州分行根据收到的开证行发送的信用证修改函电，向受益人缮制信用证修改通知书。

Amendment to a Documentary Credit

SENDER'S REF ∗20：273637
RECEIVER'S REF ∗21：I254678
ISSUING BANK'S REF ∗23：LCBH156378
ISSUING BANK ∗52s：BANK OF CHINA，LONDON
DATE OF ISSUE 31C：960514
DATE OF AMENDMENT 30：960520
NUMBER OF AMENDMENT 26E：01
BENEFICIARY 59：GUANGZHOU ARTS & CRAFTS IMP. & EXP. CORP.，GUANGZHOU DADAO，GUANGZHOU
CHINA
NARRATIVE 79：+PARTIAL SHIPMENT NOW TO BE ALLOWED
+EXPIRY PLACE TO READ CHINA
+AMOUNT INCREASED BY USD56 000.00 TO USD60 000.00
+UNIT PRICE NOW CHANGED TO READ USD850/TON INSTEAD OF USD820/TON
YOUR ADVICE SHOULD CONFIRM DATE OF YOUR REMITTANCE OF STRICTLY COMPLYING DOCUMENTS TO US.

Trailer......

NOTIFICATION OF AMENDMENT
TO LETTER OF CREDIT

TO ____________________
(Beneficiary)

____________________ Advising Bank Ref. ____________

We received a telegram dated ____________ from ____________
(year-month-date) (issuing bank)

LC No. ____________ Amount ____________ Applicant AA Import Co.

Which is amended as follows：

–
–
–
–
–
–

All other terms and conditions remain as per the above-mentioned Letter of Credit.
The amendment is valid.

Name of Advising Bank ____________
Address ____________
Signature ____________

（六）信用证的议付、寄单索偿

根据受益人 GUANGZHOU FEI YUE SEWING MACHINE MANUFACTORY 6 月 20 日提交的议付申请书，议付行 BANK OF CHINA，GUANGZHOU 审单相符议付后，于6 月 23 日据此缮制并寄送出口寄单议付通知书向开证行索偿，开证行于 6 月 30 日据此缮制进口单到通知书。

APPLICATION FOR NEGOTIATION

To：Bank of China，GUANGZHOU　　　　No. BP346758

Date：June 20，2002

Dear Sirs,

We send you herewith for negotiation our drafts No. 893729 for USD20 000. 00（SAY US DOLLARS TWENTY THOUSAND ONLY）

Drawn under Letter of Credit No. A－01－I－70498 issued by BANK OF CHINA，NEW YORK

accompanied by the following documents：

[X] Invoice 4　　[X] Packing List 4

[X] Insurance 2　　□Consular Invoice ______

[X] Bill of Lading 3＋2（N/N）　　□Customs Invoice ______

[X] Certificate of Origin 3　　□Import License ______

□Certificate of Inspection ______　　□Letter of Transfer ______

Other documents Beneficiary's certificate 1

In consideration of your negotiation at our request the above bill（s），we undertake to hold you harmless and indemnified against any discrepancy which may cause non-payment or non-acceptance of the said draft（s），and we shall refund you in original currency the whole or party of the draft（s）amount with interest or expenses that may be accrued or incurred in connection with the above upon receipt of your notice to that effect.

In consideration of your so doing we hereby agree to accept above mentioned terms and condition.

In case of questions,

please contact Mr. 李林　　　　GUANGZHOU FEI YUE SEWING MACHINE MANUFACTORY

____

Authorized Signature

中国银行

BANK OF CHINA, GUANGZHOU

出口寄单议付通知书

When corresponding,
Please always quote → **BP NO.**

To:

We hereby certify that we have negotiated the documents under the following L/C in accordance with the terms and conditions thereof:

Draft/Inv. No.	Tenor	Amount	Our Charges	Total
	Sight		Advising of transmission Commission: Negotiation or payment Commission: Postage: Amendment Commission: Confirmation Commission:	

L/C issued by: Your Goodselves

The relative documents are disposed as follows:

DOCUMENT	Combined Form (marked X)	Com./Cust. Invoice	Manuf. Invoice	Packing Wt. Spec. List	Origin Cert.	Quanlity Analysis Cert.	Quantity Weight Cert.	Veter. Health Cet.	Ins. Cert.	Bills of Lading	N/N Bill of Lading	Cable/Letter Copy	Postal Cert.
FIRST MAIL													
SECOND MAIL													

In reimbursement, we have claimed to

We are holding a negotiating bank's/shipper's guarantee which we join and extend to you, covering the following discrepancies. (If described hereunder).
Please advise us when we may release the guarantee.

□Please remit the proceeds to us by cable under advice to us.
□Please remit the proceeds to our account with our New York agency by cable under cable advice to us.
□In reimbursement, we have debited your account with us.
□Please credit our general office account with you under cable advice to us.

GENERAL INSTRUCTION

1. Please send us payment/credit advice by airmail.
2. In case of non-acceptance/non-payment, please hold the bills protested and attend to the warehousing and fire insurance under cable advice to us giving reasons.
3. We hereby certify that the documents presented within the expiry date of the credit and/or the last day of the period of time after date of issuance of the transport document (s).

BANK OF CHINA, GUANGZHOU

Authorized Signature

进口单到通知书

Date:

<table>
<tr><td rowspan="2">Drawee:</td><td>Contract No.</td><td></td></tr>
<tr><td>Our L/C Bill No.</td><td></td></tr>
<tr><td rowspan="3">Drawer:</td><td>Draft Amount</td><td></td></tr>
<tr><td>Exchange Rate</td><td></td></tr>
<tr><td>Equivalent RMB</td><td></td></tr>
<tr><td>Negotiated/Presented by:</td><td>Tenor/Due date</td><td></td></tr>
<tr><td>Their Ref. No. Dated</td><td colspan="2">Documents as per copy of the presenting bank's covering letter unless otherwise mentioned.</td></tr>
<tr><td colspan="3">Covering shipment of:

As per invoice No.</td></tr>
<tr><td colspan="3">Remarks/Discrepany (ies), if any (备注或不符事项):

– our commission and charges for your account.</td></tr>
<tr><td>PLEASE FOLLOW INSTRUCTIONS MARKED (X)
☐ 单已议付，请从速赎单办妥付汇手续。
☐ 鉴于汇票承兑到期，请即签回汇票。
☐ 自此通知日起三日内如无异议，我行即对外付汇。
☐ 以上不符事项如果接受，三日内签回第三联或汇票，否则视同你公司不接受不符点并通知议付行。</td><td colspan="2">BANK OF CHINA NEW YORK BRANCH

____
Authorized Signature</td></tr>
</table>

五、结果分析

1. 信用证申请书填写的完整性与准确性分析。
2. 信用证缮制的正确性和明确性分析。
3. 信用证操作流程的准确性与高效性分析。

实验五

信用证的种类

一、实验目的

1. 把握各类信用证的填写和审核。
2. 即期付款、延期付款、承兑、议付信用证的操作处理。
3. 可转让信用证的特殊操作处理。
4. 对背信用证的特殊操作处理。
5. 预支信用证的特殊操作处理。
6. 对开信用证的特殊操作处理。

二、实验原理

信用证的种类见图 5－1。

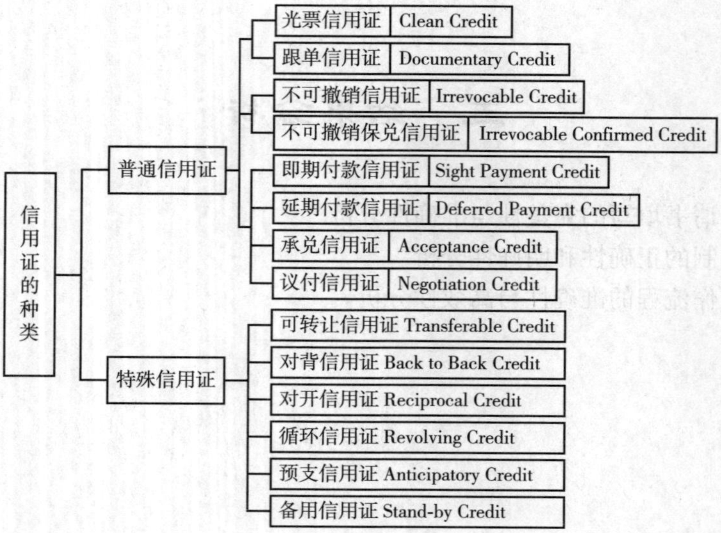

图 5－1　信用证的种类

如图 5－1 所示，信用证可分为普通信用证和特殊信用证。一张信用证从不同的角度可归属于不同的种类，如：国际贸易结算中常见的是跟单、不可撤销的议付信用证。特殊信用证与普通信用证的不同主要体现在适用的贸易背景和处理流程中的差异上。

（一）普通信用证知识点

开证行开立信用证时，都会对其种类有明确的表示。普通信用证的特点见表 5－1。

表 5－1　普通信用证特点

种　类	特　点
光票信用证	非贸易结算中使用，不附带全套商业单据，金额较小。
跟单信用证	贸易结算中使用，附带全套商业单据，涉及审单的处理。
不可撤销信用证	开证行承担第一付款责任。
不可撤销保兑信用证	开证行和保兑行同时承担第一付款责任。
即期付款信用证	审单相符，即期付款。
延期付款信用证	审单相符，延期付款。
承兑信用证	审单相符，承兑汇票，远期付款。受益人可将承兑汇票贴现，提前获得票款。
议付信用证	审单相符，即期议付买单。

UCP600 第三条规定：信用证是不可撤销的，即使未如此表明。相对于 UCP500 相关条款的规定，UCP600 进一步明确了信用证的不可撤销性。UCP600 第六条 b 款规定：任何信用证均须明确表示它适用于即期付款、延期付款、承兑抑或议付。按付款方式不同进行划分的四类信用证处理的差异见表 5－2。

表 5－2　不同付款方式信用证处理的差异

种类 / 条件	即期付款信用证	延期付款信用证	承兑信用证	议付信用证	
				限制	自由
汇票	需要或不要	不要	需要	需要或不要	
汇票期限	即期	……	远期	即期或远期	
受票人	指定付款行	……	指定承兑行	议付行以外的银行	
付款给受益人的时间	即期付款	延期付款	远期付款	扣减利息，即期付款	
起算日	……	交单日、提单日	承兑日	……	
追索权	无	无	无	有	

如表 5－2 所示，开证行开立上述四种信用证时，应在信用证中进行批注。如：一张由通知行作为指定付款行、以开证行为汇票付款人的即期付款信用证格式见示样 5－1。

示样 5－1　即期付款信用证

Credit available with <u>Advising Bank</u> by

[X] Sight payment

□Deferred payment

□Acceptance at ______ days after sight

□Negotiable

Against the documents detailed herein:

[X] And beneficiary's draft at <u>sight</u> ______ drawn on <u>Issuing Bank</u>

（二）特殊信用证知识点

1. 可转让信用证（Transferable Credit）

可转让信用证指可应受益人（第一受益人）的要求转为全部或部分由另一受益人（第二受益人）兑用的信用证。可转让信用证处理基本程序见图 5－2。

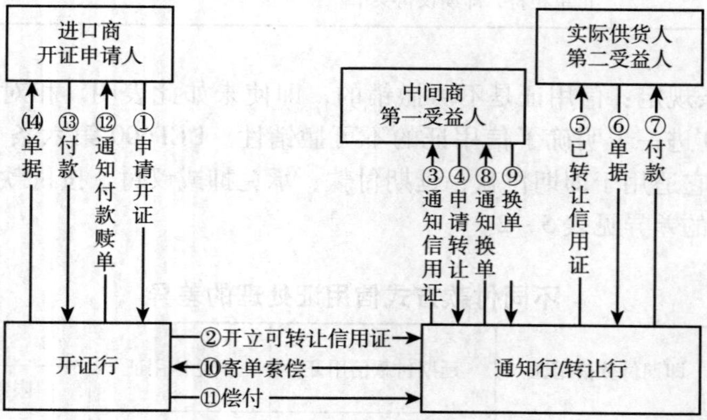

图 5－2　可转让信用证基本程序

如图 5－2 所示，可转让信用证与普通信用证的差异主要体现在：（1）适用于有中间商的贸易背景；（2）增加了信用证转让环节的处理；（3）增加了换单环节的处理。此外，在其他各环节的处理上，可转让信用证与普通信用证处理并无差异。UCP600 第三十八条对可转让信用证作了明确规定，可转让信用证处理中的具体要求见图 5－3。

2. 对背信用证（Back to Bank Credit）

对背信用证处理基本程序见图 5－4。

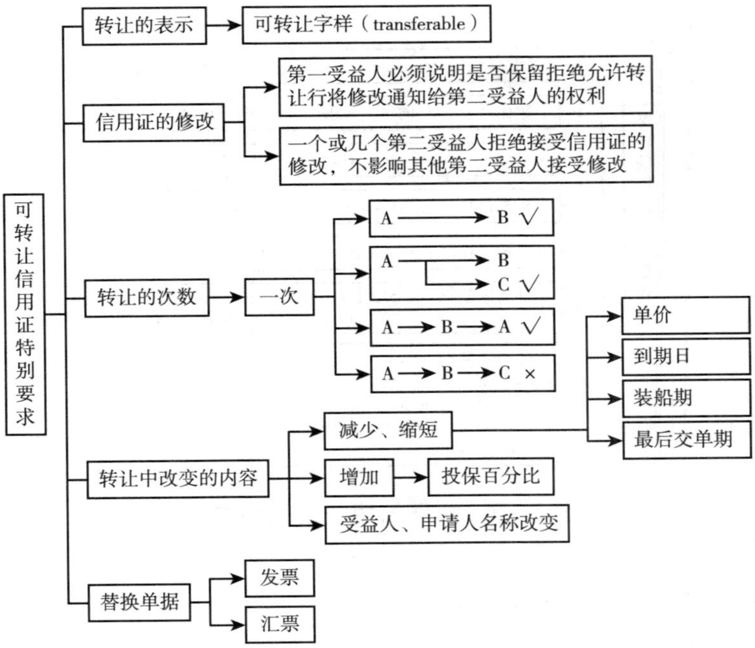

图 5－3　可转让信用证处理要求

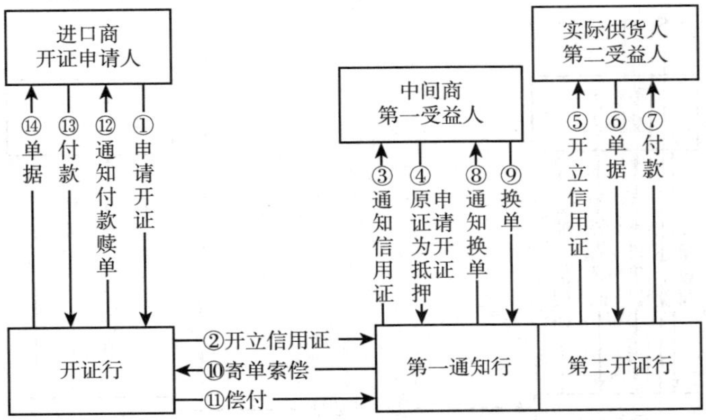

图 5－4　对背信用证处理基本程序

如图 5－4 所示，对背信用证适用于有中间商的贸易背景，涉及重新开立信用证和换单环节的处理，其中，信用证改变的内容和替换单据的种类与可转让信用证相似。但是两种信用证在开证行的责任和信用证的表示上不同。

3. 循环信用证（Revolving Credit）

循环信用证指信用证金额被全部或部分使用后，仍然恢复到原金额，可多次使用的信用证。循环信用证适用于买卖双方订立长期合同，分批交货，而且是货物比较大宗、单一的情况下，进口方为了节省开证手续和费用而采用的方法。循环信用证的循环方式见图 5－5。

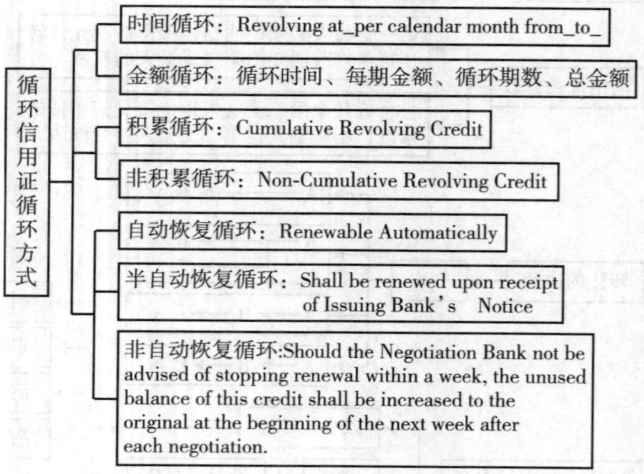

图 5－5　循环信用证的循环方式

4. 预支信用证（Anticipatory Credit）

预支信用证指开证行在信用证上加列预支条款，授权指定议付行在收到信用证后预先垫付信用证金额的一部分，用于出口商的备货装运。待出口商交单请求议付时，以议付款项偿还垫款议付行本息。预支信用证亦称红条款信用证，因预支条款一般用红色打印。预支信用证处理基本程序见图 5－6。

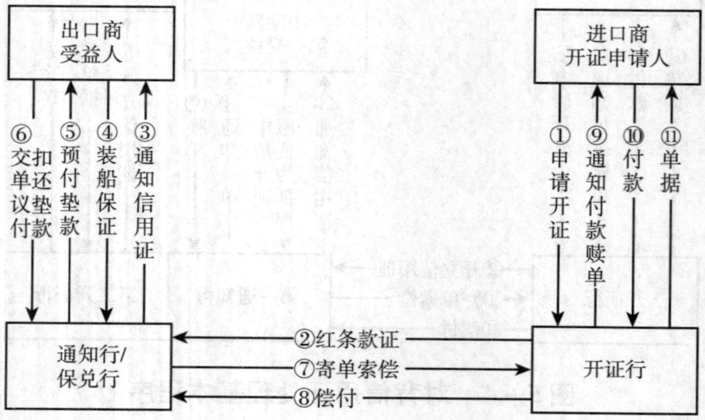

图 5－6　预支信用证处理基本程序

如图 5－6 所示，预支信用证处理中，开证行授权出口地银行凭信用证和装船保证可提前预支部分金额给出口商，从而改变了普通信用证下银行凭相符单据付款的条件。预支信用证的预支条款格式见示样 5－2。

示样 5 – 2　预支信用证

We (Issuing Bank) hereby authorize the Nominated Bank at their discretion to grant to you an advance to the extent of AUD25 000 being 80% of the Credit amount against the presentation of sight draft and undertaking of shipment. Any interest accrued thereon should be charged to you from the date of advanced draft to the date of repayment at the current rate of interest in Australia. The proceeds of any draft negotiated under the Credit may be at their discretion be applied by them in the repayment to them of the whole or any part of such advance together with interest as aforesaid.

In consideration of the Nominated Bank making such advance(s) to you and in case you will eventually fail to effect shipment covered by the credit, we guarantee repayment and undertake to pay them on demand any sum owing by you in respect of such advance(s) together with interest thereon.

5. 对开信用证 (Reciprocal Credit)

对开信用证指第一张信用证的受益人，就是第二张信用证（亦称回头证）的开证申请人；第一张信用证的通知行往往就是回头证的开证行，且两证金额大体相同。对开信用证适用于补偿贸易和易货贸易，涉及两张信用证的处理。对开信用证处理基本程序见图 5 – 7。

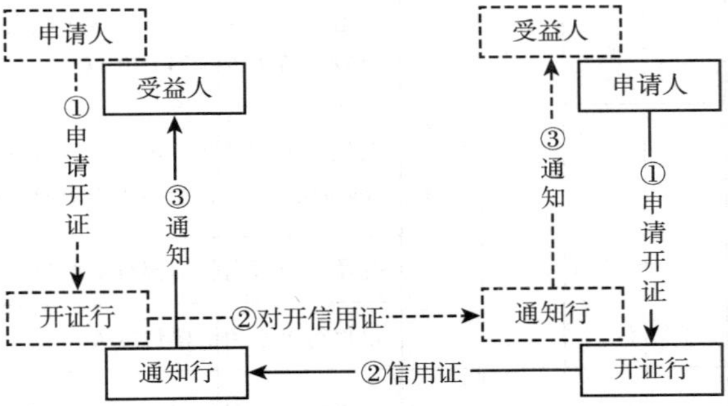

图 5 – 7　对开信用证基本程序

三、实验内容

1. 结合 UCP600 条款进行不可撤销信用证的处理。
2. 结合 UCP600 条款进行即期付款信用证的处理。
3. 结合 UCP600 条款进行延期付款信用证的处理。
4. 结合 UCP600 条款进行承兑信用证的处理。
5. 结合 UCP600 条款进行议付信用证的处理。
6. 结合 UCP600 条款进行循环信用证的处理。
7. 根据所给可转让信用证和转让申请书开立已转让信用证。

四、实验步骤

通知行收到下列各类信用证后，根据所给问题对其进行审核和处理。

审核 类型	内容					寄单	问题
	当事人	运输情况	货物情况	单据要求	效期金额		
不可撤销即期付款信用证							若受益人提交已装船提单的签发日为 2002 年 8 月 27 日，受益人于 2002 年 9 月 14 日交单。开证行能否接受该套单据？
承兑信用证							汇票承兑后至最终付款过程一般应如何处理？
延期付款信用证							若信用证由通知行保兑，当受益人交单给保兑行要求付款时，保兑行提出应由开证行先付款，只有在开证行无力付款时，保兑行才承担付款责任。该说法是否正确？
							受益人交单时，开证行能否接受注明货物数量为 41 500PCS，货物总价为 USD24 070.00 的商业发票？
议付信用证							若信用证中注明“negotiation under this credit is restricted to the advising bank”，受益人交单时应特别注意什么？
							受益人能否向任何银行交单议付？
							议付行可否为汇票付款人？
循环信用证							信用证循环的时间、使用的期数、每期金额、总金额有何规定？
							若受益人在第一次交单时只收取 J￥9 500 000.00，那么在第二次交单时，汇票金额能否为 J￥10 500 000.00？
可转让信用证							第一受益人将向转让行替换什么单据？
							转让信用证中，通知行将信用证分别转让给 A、B 两个厂商，这种做法有效吗？若信用证转让给 A 厂商后，再由 A 厂商转让给 B 厂商，这种做法有效吗？若信用证转让给 A 厂商，A 厂商再转回给原证受益人，这种做法有效吗？
							转让信用证中出现的内容有修改时，若 A 厂商拒绝接受信用证修改条款，是否会影响 B 厂商对修改内容的接受？
							转让后的信用证与原证比较，哪些内容可以改变？

（一）不可撤销即期付款信用证

<table>
<tr><td colspan="2">Eximbank Ltd.
Malaysia
Golden Horse Building
Tel: 927 – 9756
Tex: 7653428
Issued Date and Place
25 June, 2002, Malaysia</td></tr>
<tr><td>Irrevocable
Documentary Credit</td><td>Credit Number
of Issuing Bank: S – 01 – 978
of Advising Bank: ND8294</td></tr>
<tr><td>Advising Bank
Development Bank,
International Trading Building
Singapore
P. O. Box 401015</td><td>Applicant
Dearmei Trading Co. Ltd. Malaysia
2nd/F, BBB Building
Box 897645</td></tr>
<tr><td>Beneficiary
Kam Dor Bo Trading Co. , Ltd
7th/F, Forrum Building
Singapore</td><td>Expiry Date
14 September, 2002
In the country of the beneficiary</td></tr>
<tr><td colspan="2">At the request of Dearmei Trading Co. Ltd, Malaysia, we open this Irrevocable Documentary Letter of Credit No. S – 01 – 978 in your favor for an amount not exceeding total of USD1 000 000 (one million United States Dollars only) available by sight payment of your drafts drawn at sight on us covering 100% invoice value accompanied by the following documents:
1. Commercial invoice in triplicate.
2. Insurance policy in duplicate covering all risks plus 10% of invoice value.
3. Full set of clean "On Board" ocean Bills of Lading made out to our order notify buyers and marked "Freight Prepaid" .
4. Certificate of Origin in duplicate.
5. Certificate of Inspection in duplicate.</td></tr>
<tr><td colspan="2">Covering shipments of:
ESP 20 kit
ESP 10 kit } In crates
ESP 10 kit
Shipment from Singapore to Malaysia CIF Malaysia Contract No. ESP 1365
Shipment must be effected not later than 30 August , 2002</td></tr>
<tr><td colspan="2">Special clause:
1. This credit is available by draft drawn on issuing bank at sight.
2. Partial shipments are prohibited.
Transshipments are prohibited.
3. All documents must be presented in 15 days after shipment but within the validity of the credit.
4. The number and date of this credit must appear on draft drawn.
5. The amount of draft must be endorsed on the back hereof and this credit is to be returned to us when exhausted or expired.
6. Draft against this credit must be drawn and negotiated on or before 14 September, 2002.</td></tr>
<tr><td colspan="2">We hereby guarantee that drafts drawn under and in compliance with the terms and conditions of this credit shall be accepted and paid at sight.

For Eximbank, Ltd.
Malaysia

____
Authorized Signature</td></tr>
</table>

（二）承兑信用证

……

We hereby establish Irrevocable Letter of Credit No. H/IA020608/02

Amount: USD59 700.00

Validity: 30 November 2009, in P. R. of China

Applicant: Helm AG, Hamburg, Germany

Beneficiary: China National Chemicals Imp. & Exp. Corp.

Available with Issuing Bank by acceptance of your draft drawn on us at 30 days after sight against presentation of the following documents:

1. Signed commercial invoice in 4-fold

2. Full set of 3/3 original plus 2/2 copies of clean on board ocean/marine Bills of Lading, originals signed, issued to order and blank endorsed, notify: Helm AG, Hamburg marked "Freight Prepaid", evidencing shipment from P. R. Chinese main port to Rotterdam not later than 15 Nov., 2009 for 60MT = 3FCL.

- Transshipment not allowed;

- Container shipment: Prescribed.

- B/L to show container No. /Nos. and to show always name, place, phone and telex-No. of the carrier.

3. Certificate of Origin, Form "A" showing P. R. of China as origin, one original and one copy, legalized by a Commodity Inspection Bureau of the P. R. of China and in accordance with rules agreed with EEC-authorities.

4. Packing/Weight list 2-fold, stating: kind, number, content, net weight, gross weight and measurements of each and total packages.

5. Certified copy of telegr. of telex advice to applicants latest 2 days after shipment, showing quantity, product, total net and gross weight, date of B/L, vessel's name, B/L No., loading port, destination port, ets. And No. 912/00700.

6. Certificate of Analysis, 2-fold, issued by the beneficiary.

Certifying: Citric Acid Anhydrous BP 80, giving full specifications

Description of goods: 60MT = 3FCL of citric acid anhydrous bp 80

China contract No.: CNC9 - B00128

Unit price: USD995, —/net CFR Rotterdam, as per incoterms 1990

Packed: in 25 kgs net multiply bags (export-and seaworthy)

Marks: citric acid anhydrous bp 80

25kgs net

Rotterdam…

Special conditions:

1. DOCUMENTS are to be presented within 15 days after Bill of Lading date.

2. This credit is subject to ICC publication No. 600.

3. All banking commissions and charges outside Germany are for account of beneficiary, also in case of non-utilization.

4. Any original documents, excl. any kind of marine Bills of Lading, produced by reprographic systems, computerized systems or carbon copies, only acceptable if they are clearly marked as "original" and signed by the issuer in handwriting.

5. Documents including transport documents dated prior to the issuance of this credit are not acceptable.

6. Partial shipment not allowed.

7. Third party transport documents are not acceptable.

8. The amount of each drawing must be endorsed on the reverse side of the original instrument.

9. Payment will only be effected after receipt of first and second mail documents.

10. Please send the documents to the following address:

DEUTSCHE BANK HAMBURG

（三）延期付款信用证

TO：THE BANK OF EAST ASIA LTD.，GUANGZHOU
FM：THE BANK OF EAST ASIA LTD.，HONG KONG
24 SEP，2000
TEST NO. 99489
ISSUED IRREVOCABLE DOCUMENTARY CREDIT 3201N05374 FOR USD23 200.00（UNITED STATES DOLLARS TWENTY THREE THOUSAND TWO HUNDRED ONLY）
BENEFICIARY：CHINA NATIONAL AUTOMOTIVE INDUSTRY IMP. AND EXP. CORP. GUANGZHOU，CHINA
APPLICANT：PREMIER BEARING AND EQUIPMENT LTD. HONG KONG
CREDIT AVAILABLE WITH US BY DEFERRED PAYMENT AT 60 DAYS B/L DATE
VALID UNTIL 15 NOV. 2000 IN HONG KONG
PARTIAL SHIPMENT：ALLOWED
TRANSSHIPMENT：NOT ALLOWED
LOADING ON BOARD/DISPATCHING /TAKING IN CHARGE OF
FROM：GUANGZHOU，CHINA
PORT OF DISCHARGE：ROTTERDAM
COUNTRY OF DESTINATION THE NETHERLANDS
NOT LATER THAN：31 OCT，2000
COVERING SHIPMENT OF：

BEARING	QTY	UNIT PRICE
255212（420205）	40，000PCS	USD0.58/PC

SHIPPING MARK：P.O. 757/92/10
NO. 1－UP
PRICE TERM：CIF HONG KONG
TO BE ACCOMPANIED BY THE FOLLOWING DOCUMENTS：
－SIGNED COMMERCIAL INVOICE IN THREE ORIGINAL.
－COMPLETE SET CLEAN RAILWAY CARGO RECEIPT PLUS ONE NON-NEGOTIABLE COPY ISSUED OR ENDORSED TO THE ORDER OF THE BANK OF EAST ASIA，LTD.，NOTIFY APPLICANT AND MARKED FREIGHT PREPAID AND THIS CREDIT NUMBER.
－INSURANCE POLICY OR CERTIFICATE IN DUPLICATE BLANK ENDORSED FOR 110 PCT OF INVOICE VALUE WITH CLAIMS PAYABLE AT DESTINATION IN THE SAME CURRENCY OF THIS CREDIT WITH LOCAL CLAIMS AGENTS NAME AND ADDRESS AT DESTINATION COVERING INSTITUTE CARGO CLAUSE（A），INSTITUTE CARGO CLAUSE（WAR）AND MARINE TRANSPORTATION ALL RISKS，INCLUDING WAREHOUSE TO WAREHOUSE RISKS AND F.R.E.C.，SHORTAGE，TPND OF AN ENTIRE PACKAGE，BUNDLE，BAG OF PIECE.
－PACKING LIST IN TRIPLICATE INDICATING PALLET NO. OR CASE NO.，QTY OF EACH PACKAGE，QTY OF EACH PALLET OR QTY OF EACH CASE AND NET WEIGHT AND MEASUREMENT OF EACH PACKAGE.
－BENEFICIARY'S DECLARATION DECLARE THE BRAND NAME AND PACKING（EITHER IN ROLL/EACH IN INNER BOX/WITHOUT INNER BOX）OF EACH BEARING.
－BENEFICIARY'S CERTIFIED COPY OF TELEX/FAX ADVICE DESPATCHED TO APPLICANT WITHIN THREE DAYS AFTER SHIPMENT ADVISING NAME OF TERMINAL，DEPARTURE DATE，TRAIN NUMBER，PACKING DETAILS，ITEM NO.，BRAND NAME，GROSS AND NET WEIGHT AND MEASUREMENT OF EACH PACKAGE，TOTAL QUANTITY，UNIT PRICE OF EACH ITEM，PIECES PER CASE AND VALUE OF GOODS.
－CERTIFICATE OF ORIGIN FORM A IN ONE ORIGINAL AND ONE COPY SHOWING GOODS CONSIGNED.
CONFIRMATION：CONFIRMATION
ALL DOCUMENTS MUST BE PRESENTED THRU YOUR BANKER WITHIN 15 DAYS AFTER THE DATE OF ISSUANCE OF THE TRANSPORT DOCUMENT（S）BUT WITHIN THE VALIDITY OF THE CREDIT.
ADDITIONAL CONDITIONS：
－SHIPMENT EFFECTED PRIOR TO DATE OF ISSUANCE OF THIS CREDIT UNACCEPTABLE.
－A TOLERANCE OF 5PCT MORE OR LESS IN QUANTITY FOR EACH ITEM IS PERMITTED AND THE VALUE OF THIS CREDIT MAY BE ADJUSTED ACCORDINGLY.
－ALL BANKING CHARGES OUTSIDE HONG KONG ARE FOR BENEFICIARY'S ACCOUNT.
－FOR EACH PRESENTATION OF DISCREPANT DOCUMENTS UNDER THIS DOCUMENTARY CREDIT，A FEE OF USD30.00（OR EQUIVALENT）SHOULD BE DEDUCTED FROM THE REIMBURSEMENT CLAIM，NOTWITHSTANDING ANY INSTRUCTION TO THE CONTRARY，THIS CHARGE SHOULD BE FOR ACCOUNT OF BENEFICIARY.
－DISCOUNT CHARGES（INTEREST）ARE FOR ACCOUNT OF BENEFICIARY.
－ALL DOCUMENTS MUST BE FORWARDED TO US IN TWO CONSECUTIVE AIRMAILS TOGETHER WITH YOUR CERTIFICATION THAT THE AMOUNT DRAWING HAD BEEN ENDORSED ON THE REVERSE SIDE HEREOF.

THIS CREDIT IS ISSUED SUBJECT TO THE RULES OF THE UNIFORM CUSTOMS AND PRACTICE FOR DOCUMENTARY CREDIT OF THE INTERNATIONAL CHAMBER OF COMMERCE，PARIS CURRENTLY IN FORCE ON DATE OF ISSUANCE AND ENGAGES US IN ACCORDANCE WITH THE TERMS HEREOF.
THE NUMBER AND DATE OF THE CREDIT AND THE NAME OF OUR BANK MUST BE QUOTED ON ALL DRAFTS REQUIRED.
THIS IS AN OPERATIVE CREDIT INSTRUMENT AND NO AIRMAIL CONFIRMATION WILL BE FOLLOWED.

THE BANK OF EAST ASIA LTD. HONG KONG

（四）议付信用证

Commercial Development Bank Telephone: 288514 Telex: 42515SC **Original** Date: 10 April, 2000	
IRREVOCABLE **DOCUMENTARY CREDIT**	Credit Number SHI1002
Advising Bank Commercial Bank Golden Commercial Building 522A Nathan Road Kowloon, Hong Kong	Applicant Baodeli Communication Equipment Industry Co. Ltd. P. O. Box 2356 Colombo Lanka
Beneficiary Celebrity International Trading Co. Ltd. 152 Lock Road, Hong Kong	AmountUSD100 000.00 (One hundred thousand U. S. Dollars) Expiry Date: 8 June, 2000 at the counter of: advising bank

Dear Sir(s),

We hereby issue in your favor this documentary credit which is available with any bank by negotiation of your draft(s) at 30 days after sight accompanied by the following documents marked with "X":

[X] Commercial invoice in duplicate

[X] Packing list in duplicate

[X] Certificate of Origin in triplicate

[X] Full set clean "On board" ocean Bills of Lading made out to our order notify buyer and marked "Freight Prepaid"

Covering shipments of:
SQE－TYPE Ⅱ x 10 Contract No. Q521SH in wooden cases.

Latest shipment is until: 24 May, 2000
From : Hong Kong to Colombo

Partial shipment: [ ] Allowed [X] Not allowed   Transshipment: [ ] Allowed [X] Not allowed

Documents must be presented for negotiation within 15 days after B/L date in any event within the validity of the credit.

We hereby engages that drafts drawn in conformity with the terms of this credit will be duly accepted on presentation and duly honored at maturity.

Yours faithfully

Commercial Development Bank

Authorized Signature

（五）循环信用证

<table>
<tr><td>Irrevocable Documentary Credit
REVOLVING
NON-ACCUMULATIVE</td><td>Date and place of expiry：
30 September，2002
In the country of beneficiary</td></tr>
<tr><td>Applicant
JOAN'S BOUTIQUE
DISTRIBUTION CORP.
14 FAT TAT ROAD
LOWLOON，HONG KONG</td><td>Beneficiary
SUSI TRADING LTD.
60 KANGISO
TOKYO，JAPAN</td></tr>
<tr><td>Advising Bank
MITSUBISHI BANK LTD.
3，CHIYODA－KU
TOKYO，JAPAN</td><td rowspan="2">Amount：J￥10 000 000.00
(JAPANESE YEN TEN MILLION ONLY)
PER CALENDER MONTH
COMMERNCIING 19 APRIL，2002</td></tr>
<tr><td>Partial shipments
[X] allowed □not allowed</td></tr>
<tr><td>Transshipment
[X] allowed □not allowed</td><td rowspan="2">Credit available with ADVISING BANK
[X] by sight payment
□by acceptance
□by negotiation
□by deferred payment at
against the documents detailed herein：
[X] and beneficiary's draft at sight
drawn on APPLICANT</td></tr>
<tr><td>Loading on board/dispatch from
TOKYO
for transportation to：HONG KONG
LATEST 9 SEPTEMBER，2002</td></tr>
<tr><td colspan="2">－Signed Commercial Invoice in three copies certifying that the goods are in accordance with purchase order number 7086.
－Full set of clean on board marine Bill of Lading made out to shipper's order blank endorsed marked "Freight Collect" notify applicant with full address.
－Certificate of Origin in three copies.
－Inspection Certificate issued by applicant prior to shipment in one original.
－Packing List in three copies.
Covering 250 sets JAPANESE CHILDREN GARMENTS J￥40 000.00 per set FOB TOKYO
Special condition：This credit is revolving at J￥10 000 000.00 covering shipment of 6 per calendar month non-cumulative operation from April 2002 to September 2002 inclusive up to a total of J￥60 000 000.00</td></tr>
<tr><td colspan="2">Documents to be presented within 21 days after the date of issuance of the transport document (s) but within the validity of the credit.</td></tr>
<tr><td colspan="2">We hereby issue the Documentary Credit in your favor. It is subject to the Uniform Customs and Practice for Documentary Credits (1993 Revision，International Chamber of Commerce，Paris，France，and Publication No. 500) and engages us in accordance with the terms thereof. The number and the date of the credit and the name of our bank must be quote on all drafts required. If the credit is available by negotiation，each presentation must be noted on the reverse of this advice of the bank where the credit is available.
STANDARD CHARTERED BANK LTD. HONG KONG

____
Authorized Signature</td></tr>
</table>

（六）可转让信用证

2003 年 8 月 17 日，受益人 KENNY INTERNATIONAL CO. LTD.，HONG KONG 根据收到的如下信用证，向转让行 BANK OF EAST ASIA HONG KONG 填写转让申请书，开证行据此缮制一份已转让信用证。

FM FIRST NATIONAL BANK OF BOSTON, MONTEVIDEO, URUGUAY
TO BANK OF EAST ASIA HONG KONG
FORM OF D/C: IRREVOCABLE TRANSFERABLE
DOC CREDIT NO.: GH 9136127
DATE OF ISSUE: 08132003
EXPIRY DATE: 20031102, THE COUNTER OF BEA HONG KONG
APPLICANT: GERADO NOCETTI MONTEVIDEO
BENEFICIARY: KENNY INTERNATIONAL CO. LTD. HONG KONG
CURRE. AMOUNT: USD60 000.00
AVAILABLE WITH BANK OF: WITH ANY BANK BY NEGOTIATION
DRAFTS: AT SIGHT
DRAWN ON: FIRST NATIONAL BANK OF BOSTON, MONTEVIDEO, URUGUAY
PARTIAL SHIP: ALLOWED
TRANSSHIPMENT: ALLOWED
TRANSPORT FROM: ASIAN PORT
TRANSPORT TO: MONTEVIDEO URUGUAY
LATEST: 10122003
GOODS DESCRIPTION: AS PER S/C NO. 89765 CONTAINERS CIF MONTEVIDEO
25 000KGS USD2.4/KG TOTAL: USD60 000
DOCUMENTS:
- INVOICE IN 4 COPIES EVIDENCING FOB INSURANCE/FREIGHT VALUES SEPARATELY.
- INSURANCE POLICY OR CERTIFICATE IN DUPLICATE COVERING 110% OF INVOICE AMOUNT, COVERING ALL RISKS.
- FULL SET OF CLEAN ON BOARD OCEAN BILLS OF LADING MADE OUT TO ORDER, NOTIFY: GERADO NOCETTI MARKED FREIGHT PAID.
- PACKING LIST IN 1 COPY.
- CONTAINERS MUST BE SHIPPED HOUSE TO HOUSE, THE CARRIAGE FROM PORT TO WAREHOUSE IS FOR APPLICANT'S ACCOUNT AND LC CONFIRMATION FEE FOR APPLICANT'S ACCOUNT.
- THIRD PARTY SHIPPER IS ACCEPTABLE.
- DRAFT MUST SHOW NUMBER OF LC N NAME OF ISSUING BANK.
PERIOD PRESENT: 21 DAYS AFTER SHIPMENT.
CHARGES: DISCREPANCY FEES (IF ANY) USD25 ARE FOR BEN'S A/C.
REIMB BANK: THE FIRST NATIONAL BANK OF BOSTON, MASSACHUSETTS, USA.
CONFIRMATION: CONF.
INSTRUCT PAY: THREE WORKING DAYS AFTER YOUR TESTED TELEX TO US ADVISING NEGOTIATION OF DOCUMENTS STRICTLY COMPLYING WITH LC TERMS YOU MAY CLAIM REIMBT. FM NOMINATED REIMB. BANK.
OTHER TERMS AND CONDITIONS: ……
THIS CREDIT IS SUBJECT TO UCP ICC PUBL. 500, NO MAIL CONFIRMATION WILL FOLLOW

FIRST NATIONAL BANK OF BOSTON
MONTEVIDEO, URUGUAY

APPLICATION FOR TRANSFER

TO: BANK OF EAST ASIA HONG KONG

Dated: 17 August, 2003

Dear Sirs,

Re: Credit No. 36127 dated 13 August, 2003

Issued by FIRST NATIONAL BANK OF BOSTON, MONTEVIDEO, URUGUAY

For account of: GERADO NOCETTI

1. (A) Without any engagement on your part, please transfer the above-mentioned credit to FIRECRACKERS N FIREWORKS IMP. N EXP. CORP. 235 XX ROAD, GUANGZHOU CHINA on the same terms and conditions with exception of the following:

① Our name is to be substituted for the account party mentioned above.

② Amount (in words and figures): USD56, 400.00 (Fifty six thousand four hundred US dollars).

③ Unit price: USD2.256/KG.

④ Insurance for 117.02% of the invoice value.

⑤ Latest shipment date: 10012003

⑥ Expiry date: 10222003

(B) Upon payment by you of any draft under the transferred credit, or at any time on your demand, we shall deliver to you our draft and commercial invoices drawn in accordance with the original Documentary Credit in order that these documents may be substituted for the transferee's draft and invoices, the latter of which are to be delivered to us together with your payment for the difference between the two invoices, less any charges due to you. In addition to our draft and invoices we also undertake to deliver to you any other documents which may be needed to substitute for any of the transferee's documents, which do not comply as regards value etc. with the requirements of the original credit. Should we fail, at your demand, to deliver to you immediately the new drafts, invoices, and any other documents required as specified above, you are authorized to dispose the invoices and other documents accompanying the draft of the transferee to your principals without any responsibility on your part for payment of any difference between the amount of the transferee's draft and amount authorized to be paid under the original Documentary Credit.

2. Any alterations/amendments to the Credit which may be sent to us will be passed on to you for your notification to the new beneficiary.

3. We agree to be charged with interest for the period, if any, from the date of your payment to the transferee up to the date of payment of the documents under the original Documentary Credit, and with any charges incurred by you or your correspondents in connection with this transferred credit.

4. Neither you nor your correspondents shall be responsible for description, quantity, quality or value of the merchandise, shipped under the transferred Documentary Credit, nor for the correctness, genuineness of validity of the documents, nor for any other cause beyond your or their control.

5. The original advice of the Credit is submitted to you herewith and we shall be glad if you will notify the new beneficiary at our expense by:

☐ Airmail ☐Brief cable with details to follow by airmail ☒ Full cable/telex

Yours faithfully

FOR & ON BEHALF OF

KENNY INTERNATIONAL CO. LTD. HONG KONG

Authorized Signature

TRANSFERRED CREDIT

FM: BANK OF EAST ASIA LIMITED HONG KONG
TO: BANK OF EAST ASIA GUANGZHOU
DD 19 AUG 2003 TEST...
WITHOUT ANY RESPONSIBILITY OR ENGAGEMENT ON OUR PART AT THE REQUEST OF ________
________, WE HEREBY TRANSFER PART OF THE ________
______ LC NO. ________ DATED ________ UNDER OUR TRANSFER REF 1510T03826T1 TO
______ AS FOLLOWS:
EXPIRY DATE: 10222003 AT THE COUNTER OF BEA HONG KONG
TRANSFEROR: ________
TRANSFEREE: ________

CURR. AMOUNT: ________
AMOUNT SPECI: NOT EXCEEDING
AVAILABLE WITH BANK OF: WITH BEA HONG KONG BY PAYMENT
DRAFTS AT:
DRAWN ON:
PARTIAL SHIPMENT:
TRANSSHIPMENT:
TRANSPORT FROM:
TRANSPORT TO:
LATEST:
GOODS DESCRIP:
DOCUMENTS:
-
-
-
-
ADD. CONDITION:
-
-
-

CHARGES:
REIMB BANK:
CONFIRMATION:
INSTRUCT PAY:
THIS CREDIT IS SUBJECT TO UCP ICC PUBL. 500, NO MAIL CONFIRMATION WILL FOLLOW OTHER TERMS AND CONDITIONS:
- NOTWITHSTANDING ANY INSTRUCTIONS TO THE CONTRARY THAT APPEAR IN THE FOREGOING CREDIT, DOCUMENTS TOGETHER WITH DRAFTS UNDER THIS TRANSFER OF CREDIT MUST BE PRESENTED TO BEA HONG KONG IN ONE LOT TO ARRIVE NOT LATER THAN 22 OCT, 2003 FOR SUBSTITUTION DOCUMENTS BY THE FIRST BENEFICIARY.
- DOCUMENTS ARE TO BE PRESENTED THROUGH YR BANKER AND ARE SUBJECT TO FINAL ACCEPTANCE BY THE CREDIT ISSUING BANK OR CONFIRMING BANK.
- PAYMENT WILL BE MADE IN ACCORDANCE WITH THE PRESENTING BANK'S INSTRUCTION AFTER OUR RECEIPT OF FUNDS FROM THE ISSUING BANK.
- THE PRESENTING BANK MUST QUOTE OUR TRANSFER REF. NO. 1510T03826T1 ON THEIR COVERING LETTER WHEN PRESENTING THE DOCUMENTS TO US FOR SUBSTITUTION OF DOCUMENTS BY THE FIRST BENEFICIARY WHO RESERVES THE RIGHT TO CLAIM ANY LOSSES SHOULD TRANSFEREE'S DOCUMENTS BE PRESENTED TO CREDIT ISSUING BANK DIRECTLY UNLESS THE TRANSFEROR FAILS TO SUBMIT THEIR OWN DOCUMENTS UPON FIRST DEMAND BY THE BANK DESIGNATED ABOVE.
- ALL DOCUMENTS EXCEPT DRAFTS AND INVOICES MUST NOT SHOW THE VALUE AND UNIT PRICE OF GOODS UNLESS OTHERWISE STIPULATED ON THE CREDIT.
THIS TRANSFER OF CREDIT IS SUBJECT TO UCP CURRENTLY IN FORCE AT TIME OF ISSUANCE OF THE ORIGINAL CREDIT.

BANK OF EAST ASIA LIMITED HONG KONG

五、结果分析

1. 各种类型信用证缮制的完整性与准确性分析。
2. 特殊信用证操作流程的准确性与高效性分析。

实验六

信用证中的单据

一、实验目的

1. 掌握海运提单有效性、合规性的审核。
2. 掌握保险单据有效性、合规性的审核。
3. 掌握商业发票有效性、合规性的审核。
4. 掌握汇票有效性、合规性的审核。
5. 掌握附属单据有效性、合规性的审核。
6. 掌握原产地证、包装单、质量检验证书、数量检验证书等附属单据的审核。

二、实验原理

(一) 单据审核基本原则和要求知识点

单据（Documents）也称货运单据、商业单据，是出口方应进口方和其他有关方的要求必须备妥并提交的，完整地代表货物所有权的各种货运单据。它通常是由出口方制作或取得后通过银行转交给进口方，交单是出口方履约的重要环节和内容。

1. 单据的种类

信用证中受益人提交的单据种类见图 6－1。

如图 6－1 所示，在受益人提交种类繁多的各种单据中，商业发票是全套单据的中心单据。运输单据中以海运提单居多，作为一种物权凭证，海运提单是银行审单中的一个重点。受益人是否需提交保险单据，视价格条件而定。如：CIF 价格条件下由卖方投保，须提交保险单据，FOB 价格条件下由买方投保，无须提交保险单据。是否需提交汇票视信用证的付款方式而定，承兑信用证必须提交汇票，延期付款信用证不需要汇票，即期付款和议付信用证可带汇票也可不带汇票。

2. 审核的原则和要求

除偿付行外，开证行和信用证中的指定银行都涉及审单的处理。出口地银行和开证行应根据信用证条款、《跟单信用证统一惯例》（UCP600）和《关于审核跟单信用证项下单据的国际标准银行实务》（ISBP）来审核单据。UCP600 中有关单据审核的基本原则和要求见表 6－1。

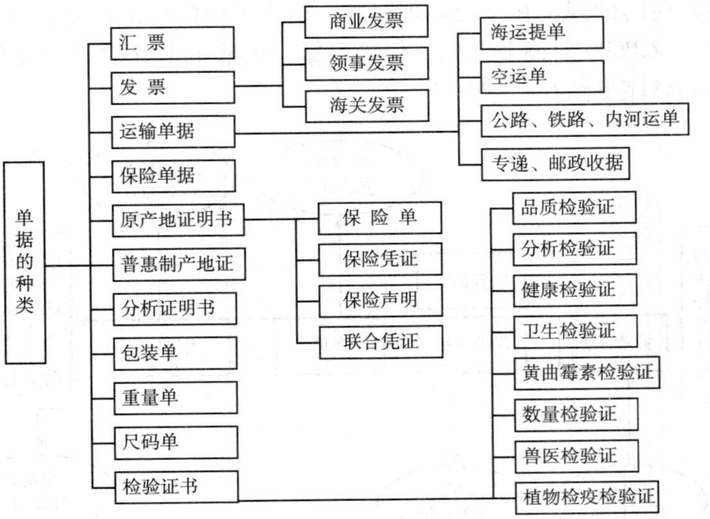

图 6－1 单据的种类

表 6－1 单据审核的基本原则和要求

项　目	UCP600	要　求
指示、行为单据化	第五条	银行处理的是单据，而不是单据可能涉及的货物、服务或履约行为。
	第十四条 g 分条	提交的非信用证所要求的单据将被不予理会，并可被退还给交单人。
	第十四条 h 分条	如果信用证含有一项条件，但未规定用以表明该条件得到满足的单据，银行将视为未作规定并不予理会。
签发人	第三条	用诸如“第一流的”、“著名的”、“合格的”、“独立的”、“正式的”、“有资格的”或“本地的”等词语描述单据的出单人时，允许除受益人之外的任何人出具该单据。
正副本单据	第十七条 b 分条	银行应将任何带有看似出单人的原始签名、标记、印戳或标签的单据视为正本单据，除非单据本身表明其非正本。
	第十七条 c 分条	除非单据本身另有说明，以下情况，银行也将其视为正本单据： ⅰ. 单据看似由出单人手写、打字、穿孔或盖章；或者 ⅱ. 单据看似使用出单人的原始信纸出具；或者 ⅲ. 单据声明其为正本单据，除非该声明看似不适用于提交的单据。
	第十七条 d 分条	假如信用证要求提交单据的副本，提交正本或副本均可。
	第十七条 e 分条	假如信用证使用诸如“一式两份（in duplicate）”、“两份（in two fold）”、“两套（in two copies）”等用语要求提交多份单据，则提交至少一份正本，其余使用副本即可满足要求，除非单据本身另有说明。
签字	第三条	单据签字可用手签、摹样签字、穿孔签字、印戳、符合或任何其他机械或电子的证实方法为之。
出单日	第十四条ⅰ分条	单据日期可以早于信用证的开立日期，但不得晚于交单日期。
	第二十八条 E 分条	保险单据日期不得晚于发运日期，除非保险单据表明保险责任不迟于发运日生效。
审单依据	第一条	《跟单信用证统一惯例——2007 年修订本，国际商会第 600 号出版物》（简称“UCP”）乃一套规则，适用于所有的其文本中明确表明受本惯例约束的跟单信用证（下称“信用证”）（在其可适用的范围内，包括备用信用证。）除非信用证明确修改或排除，本惯例各条文对信用证所有当事人均具有约束力。
	第十四条	按指定行事的指定银行、保兑行（如果有的话）及开证行须审核交单，并仅基于单据本身确定其是否在表面上构成相符交单。
交单时间	第三十三条	银行在其营业时间外无接受交单的义务。
审单时间	第十四条 b 分条	按指定行事的指定银行、保兑行（如有的话）及开证行各有从交单次日起至多五个银行工作日用以确定交单是否相符。这一期限不因在交单日当天或之后信用证截止日或最迟交单日截止而受到缩减或影响。

信用证中涉及时间的规定在多处体现，如：信用证中的开证日期、有效期、交单期，货物的最迟装运日。UCP600 对商业发票、保险单据、运输单据开立日和交单期也有相应的规定。单据开立时间顺序见图 6 - 2。

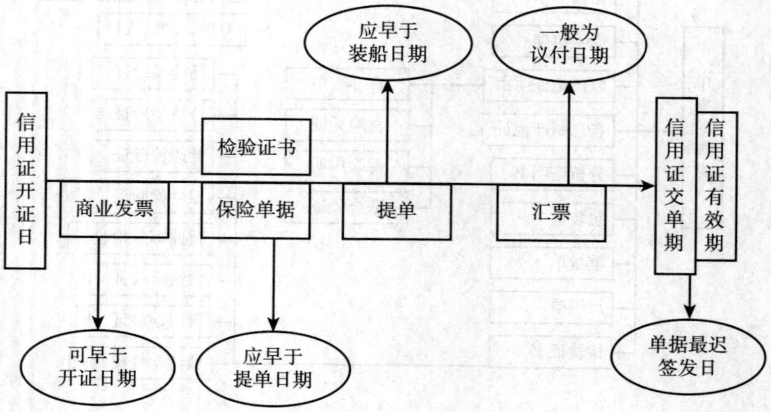

图 6 - 2　信用证下单据开立时间顺序

银行审核单据的方法和程序见图 6 - 3。

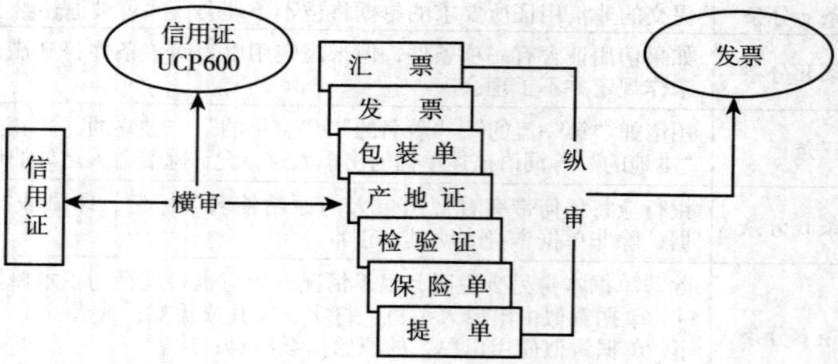

图 6 - 3　银行审核单据的方法和程序

如图 6 - 3 所示，银行审核单据时，以 UCP600 和信用证为依据，进行“单证一致”的审核，以商业发票为依据，进行“单单一致”的审核。UCP600 第四条规定，在信用证业务中，各有关当事人处理的只是单据，而不是单据所涉及的货物、服务或其他行为。银行应坚持“表面相符”的原则，只能以单证不符为理由对外拒付。在收到进口地法院止付令后，开证行也可对外拒付。此外，其他任何理由都不能成为拒付的正当理由。

（二）主要单据的审核知识点

1. 商业发票的审核（Commercial Invoice）

UCP600 中有关商业发票审核的要点见表 6 - 2。

表6－2　　　　　　　　　　**商业发票的审核要点**

<table>
<tr><th>项　目</th><th>UCP600</th><th>常见不符点</th></tr>
<tr><td>签发人签字</td><td>第十八条a分条i款规定：必须看似由受益人出具（第三十八条规定的情形除外）
iv款规定：无须签名。</td><td rowspan="2">1. 发票的货物描述与信用证不符。（Description of goods in invoice differs from that in the credit.）</td></tr>
<tr><td>抬头人</td><td>第十八条a分条ii款规定：必须出具成以申请人为抬头。（第三十八条g款规定的情形除外）</td></tr>
<tr><td rowspan="2">货币和金额</td><td>第十八条a分条iii款规定：必须与信用证的货币相同。</td><td rowspan="2">2. 发票的贸易条件不正确。（Invoice does not show correct trade terms.）</td></tr>
<tr><td>第十八条b分条规定：按指定行事的指定银行、保兑行（如有的话）或开证行可以接受金额大于信用证允许金额的商业发票，其决定对有关各方均有约束力，只要该银行对超过信用证允许金额的部分未作承付或者议付。</td></tr>
<tr><td rowspan="3">金额数量单价伸缩幅度</td><td>第三十条a分条规定：“约”或“大约”用于信用证金额或信用证规定的数量或单价时，应解释为允许有关金额或数量或单价有不超过10%的增减幅度。</td><td rowspan="2">3. 发票的参考号码与信用证不一致。（Reference number on invoice not in accordance with the credit.）</td></tr>
<tr><td>第三十条b分条规定：在信用证未以包装单位件数或货物自身件数的方式规定货物数量时，货物数量允许有5%的增减幅度，只要总支取金额不超过信用证金额。</td></tr>
<tr><td>第三十条c分条规定：如果信用证规定了货物数量，而该数量已全部发运，及如果信用证规定了单价，而该单价又未降低，或当第三十条b款不适用时，则即使不允许部分装运，也允许支取的金额有5%的减幅。若信用证规定有特定的增减幅度或使用第三十条a款提到的用语限定数量，则该减幅不适用。</td><td rowspan="2">4. 发票没有作成信用证申请人名称的抬头人。（Invoice not made out to applicant's name as shown in the credit.）</td></tr>
<tr><td>货物描述</td><td>第十八条c分条规定：商业发票上的货物、服务或履约行为的描述应该与信用证中的描述一致。</td></tr>
</table>

2. 海运提单的审核（Bill of Lading）

UCP600 中有关海运提单审核的要点见表 6－3。

表 6－3　　　　　　海运提单的审核要点

项　目	UCP600	常见不符点
签发人	第二十条 a 分条ⅰ款规定：表明承运人名称，并由下列人员签署：承运人或其具名代理人，或者船长或其具名代理人。承运人、船长或代理人的任何签字必须标明其承运人、船长或代理人的身份。代理人的任何签字必须标明其系代表承运人还是船长签字。	1. 加注条款（或不清洁）提单。（Claused or unclean Bill of Lading.）
全套正本	1. 第二十条 a 分条ⅳ款规定：为唯一的正本提单，或假如以多份正本出具，为提单中表明的全套正本。	
	2. 提单签署条款中规定：In witness whereof the Master Agent of said vessel both affirmed to <u>份数</u> Bills of Lading, all of the same tenor and date, one of which being accomplished, the other(s) to stand void.	2. 运输行发出分提单。（House Bill of Lading.）
清洁	第二十七条规定：银行只接受清洁运输单据，清洁运输单据指未载有明确宣称货物或包装有缺陷的条款或批注的运输单据。“清洁”一词并不需要在运输单据上出现，即使信用证要求运输单据为“清洁已装船”的。	3. 未能证明货物已装船。（No evidence of goods actually “shipped on board”.）
已装船	第二十条 a 分条ⅱ款规定：通过以下方式表明货物已在信用证规定的装货港装上具名船只：预先印就的文字，或已装船批注注明货物的装运日期。提单的出具日期将被视为发运日期，除非提单载有表明发运日期的已装船批注，此时已装船批注中显示的日期将被视为发运日期。	4. 提单未表明运费是否已经支付。（Bill of Lading does not evidence whether freight is paid or not.）
转运	第二十条 c 分条ⅰ款规定：提单可以表明货物将要或可能被转运，只要全程运输由同一提单涵盖。	
	第二十条 c 分条ⅱ款规定：即使信用证禁止转运，注明将要或可能发生转运的提单仍可接受，只要其表明货物由集装箱、拖车或子船运输。	
分运	第三十一条 b 分条规定：表明使用同一运输工具并经由同次航程运输的数套运输单据在同一次提交时，只要显示相同目的地，将不视为部分发运，即使运输单据上表明的发运日期不同或装货港、接管地或发运地点不同。	5. 已装船批注没有日期。（On board notation not dated.）
交单日	第十四条 c 分条规定：假如单据中包含一份或多份受第十九、二十、二十一、二十二、二十三、二十四或二十五条规制的正本运输单据，则须由受益人或其代表在不迟于本惯例所指的发运日之后的二十一个日历日内交单，但是在任何情况下都不得迟于信用证的截止日。	
不接受提单种类	第二十六条 a 分条规定：运输单据不得表明货物装于或者将装于舱面。声明可能被装于舱面的运输单据条款可以接受。	

3. 保险单据的审核（Insurance Policy/Certificate）

UCP600 中有关保险单据审核的要点见表 6－4。

表 6－4　　　　　　　　　保险单据的审核要点

项　目	UCP600	常见不符点
签发人	第二十八条 a 分条规定：保险单据，例如保险单或预约保险项下的保险证明书或者声明书，必须看似由保险公司或承保人或其代理人或代表出具并签署。	1. 提交保险单据的类型与信用证要求不符。（Presentation of an insurance document of a type other than that required by the credit.）
份数	第二十八条 b 分条规定：如果保险单据表明其以多份正本出具，所有正本均须提交。	2. 保险险别与信用证规定不符。（Insurance risks covered not as specified in the credit.）
类型及接受性	第二十八条 c 分条规定：暂保单将不被接受。	
	第二十八条 d 分条规定：可以接受保险单代预约保险项下的保险证明书或声明书。	3. 保险投保货币与信用证货币不符。（Insurance cover expressed in a currency other than that of the credit.）
签发日期	第二十八条 e 分条规定：保险单据日期不得晚于发运日期，除非保险单据表明保险责任不迟于发运日生效。	
投保币别	第二十八条 f 分条 i 款规定：保险单据必须表明投保金额并以与信用证相同的货币表示。	4. 保险金额不足。（Under-insured.）
保险金额	第二十八条 f 分条 ii 款规定：信用证对于投保金额为货物价值、发票金额或类似金额的某一比例的要求，将被视为对最低保额的要求。如果信用证对投保金额未做规定，投保金额须至少为货物的 CIF 或 CIP 价格的 110%。如果从单据中不能确定 CIF 或者 CIP 价格，投保金额必须基于要求承付或议付的金额，或者基于发票上显示的货物总值来计算，两者之中取金额较高者。	5. 保险生效日期未自提单装运日期起算。（Insurance not effective from the date of shipment on the B/L.） 6. 保险日期迟于提单装运日期。（Insurance dated later than the date of shipment on the B/L.）
投保险别	第二十八条 g 分条规定：信用证应规定所需投保的险别及附加险（如有的话）。如果信用证使用诸如“通常风险”或“惯常风险”等含义不确切的用语，则无论是否有漏保之风险，保险单据将被照样接受。	7. 保险单/保险凭证没有正确背书。（Insurance policy/certificate not endorsed correctly.）
	第二十八条 h 分条规定：当信用证规定投保“一切险”时，如保险单据载有任何“一切险”批注或条款，无论是否有“一切险”标题，均将被接受，即使其声明任何风险除外。	8. 保险单理赔地点与信用证规定不符。（Insurance policy indicating place of settling claim differs from that in the credit.）
投保区间	第二十八条 f 分条 iii 款规定：保险单据须表明承保的风险区间至少涵盖从信用证规定的货物接管地或发运地开始到卸货地或最终目的地为止。	

三、实验内容

1. 根据信用证审核汇票。
2. 根据信用证审核商业发票。
3. 根据信用证审核海运提单。

4. 根据信用证审核保险单据。
5. 根据信用证要求审核证下全套单据，提出不符点和处理建议。

四、实验步骤

（一）银行审核受益人提交的单据时，根据信用证要求和单据内容，判断哪些单据可接受，哪些不能接受，说明理由。

信用证规定	单据		接受或不接受
	种类	内 容	
About USD576 824.00	汇票	USD525 000.00	
Drawn on us		To: A Company	
Expiry date: 20 May, 2008		Issue date: 21 May, 2008	
Drawn clause		Drawn under L/C No. 12345 issued by AA Bank, dated on 15, Sept., 2008	
Commercial Invoice	商业发票	无受益人签章	
Beneficiary: A company Applicant: B company		Issuer: A company To: B company	
5 000 bags bombazine		4 950 bags bombazine	
5 000 Metric Ton peanut oil		4 692 Metric Ton peanut oil	
L/C amount: About USD100 000.00		Invoice amount: USD110 000.00 Draft amount: USD110 000.00	
L/C amount: USD100 000.00		Invoice amount: USD110 000.00 Draft amount: USD100 000.00	
Amount: USD100 000.00 39A Percentage Credit Amount Tolerance 5/5		Invoice amount: USD105 000.00 Draft amount: USD105 000.00	
Quantity: not exceeding 5 000 boxes		Quantity: 5 250 boxes	
CIFC5HongKong USD145 935.00		USD137 638.25 （总值栏金额）	
CIF Hong Kong 147 550.00, Freight fee: HKD10 560.00, Insurance fee: HKD140.00		CIF Hong Kong HKD 147 550.00 Less F HKD 10 560.00 Less F HKD 140.00 FOB HKD 136 850.00	
Marked Freight Prepaid	提单	Freight Prepayable	
Shipment not later than 20 July, 2008		备运提单签发日：“18 July, 2008”， 装船批注日期为：“22 July, 2008”	
On board Bill of Lading		On deck	

续表

信用证规定	单据		接受或不接受
	种类	内容	
Clean Bill of Lading	提单	Two bags torn	
		Used drums	
		Shipped in apparent good order and condition	
		Packaging contaminated	
		One case short shipped	
		Packaging soiled by contents	
		Insufficient packaging	
CIF New York		Freight prepaid	
CIF New York		Freight paid	
FOB New York		Freight prepaid	
CIF New York		Freight to collect	
Shipment from any port of China to New York.		Shipment from Guangzhou, to New York	
Made out to order of Issuing Bank, Issuing Bank: Standard Chartered Bank Ltd.		Consigned to: order of Issuing Bank	
Transshipment: not allowed		Shipped on board from: Guangzhou To: New York By transshipment at: Hong Kong	
Latest shipment : 15, April Expiry date: 25, April 信用证未规定交单期		提单装船日是4月3日，4月15日受益人向议付行交单议付。	
Shipped on board B/L		Received B/L	
Insurance Certificate	保险单据	Insurance Policy	
Insurance Policy		Cover Note	
Insurance policy for 110% of Invoice value, Invoice value amount USD20 000. 00		Amount insured: USD22 000. 00	
Insurance policy for 110% of Invoice value, Invoice value amount USD20 000. 00		Premium Rate: As Arranged	
Shipment not later than July, 20th, 2008		备运提单装船批注日期为："July 18th, 2008"，保险单日期为："July, 19th, 2008"。	
Covering Usual Risks		Covering All Risks and War Risks	

（二）通知行 Bank of China 根据信用证和受益人提交的全套单据，审核单据中存在的不符点并提出处理建议。

: To: 1450 14BKCHCNBJA94099065
: FM: 1550 14MTRBJPJTAXXX0694
MTRBJPJTXXX
+ MITSUI TRUST AND BANKING CO.
+ LTD. THE
+ TOKYO
: MT: 700 01
: 40A form of documentary credit: IRREVOCABLE
: 20 documentary credit number: 100934028D - 01001
: 31C date of issue: 950314
: 31D date and place of expiry: 950415 P. R. OF CHINA
: 50 applicant: SUMITOMO CORPORATION,
2 - 2 HITOTSUBASHI, CHIYODA - KU
TOKYO
: 59 beneficiary: JIANGSU NATIVE PRODUCE IMF. AND EXP. (GROUP) CORP.
36 GONG YUAN ROAD. NANJING
THE PEOPLE'S REPUBLIC OF CHINA
: 32B amount: CURRENCY JP ¥ 3 078 075. 00
: 41 - : available with /by: ANY BANK BY NEGOTIATION
: 42C: drafts at. . . : DRAFT AT 90 DAYS DATE
: 42 - : drawee: THE MITSUI TRUST AND BANKING CO. LTD.
HEAD OFFICE, TOKYO
: 43p partial shipments: PROHIBITED
: 43T transshipment: PROHIBITED
: 44A loading in charge: CHINESE AIRPORT
: 44B for transportation to: NARITA, AIRPORT
: 44C latest date of shipment: 950331
: 45A shipment of goods:
700 KGS NET OF CHINESE ROYAL JELLY (PRODUCTS
BY LAOSHAN FACTORY) IN REFRIGERATED CONTAINER
AT JP ¥ 4 510. 00 PER KG NET. LESS DISC. 2. 5%
CIF NARITA AIRPORT
: 46A: documents required:
+ SIGNED COMMERCIAL INVOICE IN QUINTUPLICATE (5) INDICATING APPLICANT'S REF NO. MCC1 - 94 - 0120 WHICH MUST BE GIVEN ON ALL OTHER DOCUMENTS
+ PACKING LIST IN DUPLICATE
+ FULL SET OF CLEAN AIR WAYBILL CONSIGNED TO SUMITOMO CORPORATION TOKYO AND MARKED FREIGHT PREPAID AND SHOWING SAME NAMES AS NOTIFY PARTY AS CONSIGNEE AND INDICATING ACTUAL FLIGHT DATE
+ FULL SET OF INSURANCE POLICIES OR CERTIFICATES ENDORSED IN BLANK, FOR 110PCT INVOICE VALUE COVERING THE INSTITUTE CARGO CLAUSES (ALL RISKS), AND THE INSTITUTE WAR CLAUSES AND THE INSTITUTE STRIKES RIOTS AND CIVIL COMMOTIONS CLAUSE AND I. O. P.
CLAIMS ARE PAYABLE IN JAPAN IN CURRENCY OF DRAFTS.
INSURANCE TO BE EFFECTED BY SHIPPER
+ ORIGINAL GSP FORM A, CERTIFICATE OF NO ANTIBIOTICS AND COPIES OF CERTIFICATE OF QUALITY ALSO REQUIRED
: 47A: additional cond. :
6) SHIPPING MARKS SHOULD INCLUDE SUMIT IN TRIANGLE.
7) TRANSPORT DOCUMENTS WHICH BEAR REFERENCE BY STAMP OF OTHERWISE TO COSTS ADDITIONAL TO THE FREIGHT ARE NOT ACCEPTABLE.
8) ORIGINAL CERTIFICATE OF QUALITY CERTIFYING PRODUCTS BY LAOSHAN FACTORY, MOISTURE MAX 67. 0PCT AND DECENOIC ACID MIN 2. 1PCT ISSUED BY C. C. I. B. SHOULD BE ATTACHED TO THE CARGO AND A BENEFICIARIE'S CERTIFICATE REQUIRED
9) DRAFT (S) TO ENFACE SAME DATE AS AIR WAYBILL AND WILL BE PAYABLE AT A FIXED DATE
: 71B: details of charges: ALL BANKING CHARGES ARE FOR ACCOUNT OF APPLICANT.
: 48: presentation period: DRAFTS/DOCUMENTS MUST BE PRESENTED WITHIN 15 DAYS AFTER DATE OF ISSUANCE OF TRANSPORT DOCUMENTS, BUT WITHIN THE VALIDITY OF CREDIT
: 49 confirmation instruction: WITHOUT
: 53 - reimbursement bank: THE MITSUI TRUST AND BANKING CO. , LTD. , HEAD OFFICE, TOKYO
: 78 instructions:
THE NEGOTIATING BANK MUST FORWARD TO US (INT'L OPERATIONS ADMINISTRATION DIV. 1 - 1 NIHONBASHI MUROMACHI 2 - CHOME. CHUO - KU TOKYO) ALL DOCUMENTS IN ONE REGISTERED AIRMAIL AND TO THE DRAWEE BANK THE DRAFTS TOGETHER WITH COMPLICANCE CERTIFICATE.
ALL DRAFTS DRAWN HERE UNDER MUST INDICATE NUMBER, DATE AND NAME OF ISSUING BANK OF THIS CREDIT.
- MAC/A1EB3306

QUINTUPLICAT

INVOICE

江苏省土产进出口集团股份有限公司

JIANGSU NATIVE PRODUCE IMPORT & EXPORT (GROUP) CORP.

38 GONG YUAN ROAD, NANJING, CHINA

TO MESSRS. DATE: MARCH 20, 1995

SUMITOMO CORPORATION
2-2 HITOTSUBASHI,
CHIYODA-KU, TOKYO, JAPAN

INVOICE NO. SU252022-J
S/C NO. 95JN1010J
L/C NO. 100934028D-01001
FROM NANJING AIRPORT TO NARITA AIRPORT

MARKS & NUMBERS
SUMIT IN TRIANGLE
SU252022-I
NARITA
NO. 1-70

ART NO. QLTY NO. DESCRIPTION	PACKAGES	QUANTITY	UNIT PRICE	AMOUNT
			CIF NARITA AIRPORT	
CHINESE ROYAL JELLY	70 CTNS.	700KGS.	@JP ¥4 510-KG NET	
DECENOIC ACID 2.151 6% MIN				JP ¥31 570 000.-
MOISTURE: 66.08% MAX			LESS 2.5% DISC.	JP ¥78 925.-

TOTAL:

PACKAGES: 70 CTNS
QUANTITY: 700 KGS NET

PRODUCTS BY LAOSHAN FACTORY
PACKING: IN 1KG/PLASTIC BOTTLE 10 KGS/CTN
THE APPLICANT'S REF NO. MCCI-94-0120

江苏省土产进出口集团股份有限公司
JIANGSU NATIVE PRODUCE
IMPORT & EXPORT (GROUP) CORP.
范 力

号码 No. SU252022 -J 南京 10 APR 1995
Nanjing

凭 不可撤销信用证
DRAWN UNDER THE MITSUI TRUST AND BANKING CO., LTD. TOKYO Irrevocable L/C No. 100934028D-01001

日期
Dated 950314

汇票金额
Exchange for JP ¥3 078 075.00

见票 日后（本汇票之副本未付）付交
At 90 DAYS sight of this FIRST of Exchange (Second of Exchange being unpaid)
Pay to the order of BANK OF CHINA

金额
the sum of JAPANESE YEN THREE MILLION SEVENTY EIGHT THOUSAND AND SEVENTY FIVE ONLY

此致
To THE MITSUI TRUST AND BANKING CO. LTD.
HEAD OFFICE, TOKYO

江苏省土产进出口集团股份有限公司
JIANGSU NATIVE PRODUCE
IMPORT & EXPORT (GROUP) CORP.
范 力

AIRPORT OF DEPARTURE NANJING FLIGHT DATE JL792 01/04/1995	AIRPORT OF DESTINATION NARITA	MASTER AIR WAYBILL NUMBER 78102730512	AIR WAYBILL NUMBER No. 0018191

ROUTING AND DESTINATION					
TO	BY FIRST CARRIEER	TO	BY	TO	BY

CONSIGNEE'S ACCOUNT NUMBER
CONSIGNEE'S NAME AND ADDRESS
SUMITOMO CORPORATION, TOKYO
2-2 HITOTSUBASHI,
CHIYODA-KU, TOKYO, JAPAN

Also NOTIFY
SUMITOMO CORPORATION,
2-2 HITOTSUBASHI,
CHIYODA-KU, TOKYO, JAPAN

SHIPPER'S ACCOUNT NUMBER
SHIPPER'S NAME AND ADDRESS

JIANGSU NATIVE PRODUCE I/E (GROUP) CORP.

NOT NEGOTIABLE
AIR WAYBILL
(AIR CONSIGNMENT NOTE)
ISSUED BY
中国对外贸易运输总公司
China National Foreign Trade
Transportation Corporation
Beijing, China
Member of FIATA

Copies 1, 2 and 3 of this Air Waybill are originals and have the same validity.

It is agreed that the goods described herein are accepted in apparent good order and condition (except as noted) for carriage SUBJECT TO THE CONDITIONS OF CONTRACT ON THE REVERSE HEREOF THE SHIPPER'S ATTENTION IS DRAWN TO THE NOTICE CONCERNING CARRIERS' LIMITATION OF LIABILITY. Shipper may increase such limitation of liability by declaring a higher value for carriage and paying a supplemental charge if required.

EXECUTED ON 30/03/1995 (Date) AT NANJING (Place)

SIGNATURE OF ISSUING CARRIER OR ITS AGENT
CHINA NATIONAL FOREIGN TRADE 李宁
TRANSPORTATION CORPORATION AS CARRIER

CURRENCY	WT/VAL		OTHER		DECLARED VALUE FOR CARRIAGE	DECLARED VALUE FOR CUSTOMS	AMOUNT OF INSURANCE	INSURANCE
JP ¥	PPD	COLL	PPD	COLL				

NO. OF PACKAGES RCP	ACTUAL GROSS WEIGHT	KG	COMMODITY ITEM NO.	CHARGEABLE WEIGHT	RATE	WEIGHT CHARGE	NATURE AND QUANTITY OF GOODS INCL. DIMENSIONS OR VOLUME:
70 CTNS	1 050 KGS		1 050KGS THE CARGO SHOULD BE KEPT -18°C DURING SHIPMENT.			JP ¥ 1 575 000.	

SPECIAL HANDLING INFORMATION INCLUDING MARKS, NUMBER AND METHOD OF PACKING.

CHINESE ROYAL JELLY
SHIPPING MARK:
SUMIT IN TRIANGLE
SU252022-J
NARITA
NO. 1-70
FREIGHT PREPAID

PREPAID	WEIGHT CHARGE JP ¥ 1 575 000. 00	OTHER CHARGES JP ¥ 23 625. 00	TOTAL OTHER CHARGES	
	VALUATION CHARGE			
COLLECT	WEIGHT CHARGE		TOTAL PREPAID JP ¥ 1 598 625. 00	TOTAL OTHER CHARGES TOTAL COLLECT
	VALUATION CHARGE			

TRIPLICATE

中 国 人 民 保 险 公 司

中 国 人 民 保 险 公 司 （ 以 下 简 称 “ 本 公 司 ” ）
THIS POLICY ON INSURANCE WITNESSES THAT THE PEOPLE'S INSURANCE COMPANY OF CHINA (HEREINAFTERCALLED "THE COMPANY")
根据
AT THE REQUEST OF JIANGSU NATIVE PRODUCE IMPORT & EXPORT (GROUP) CORP.
（ 以 下 简 称 被 保 险 人 ） 的 要 求 ， 由 被 保 险 人 向 本 公 司 缴 付 约
(HEREINAFTER CALLED "THE INSURED") AND IN CONSIDERATION OF THE AGREED PREMIUM PAID TO THE COMPANY BY THE
定 的 保 险 费 ， 按 照 本 保 险 单 承 保 险 别 和 背 面 所 载 条 款 与 下 列
INSURED UNDERTAKES TO INSURE THE UNDERMENTIONED GOODS IN TRANSPORTATION SUBJECT TO THE CONDITION OF THIS POLICY
特 款 承 保 下 述 货 物 运 输 保 险 ， 特 立 本 保 险 单 。
AS PER THE CLAUSES PRINTED OVERLEAF AND OTHER SPECIAL CLAUSES ATTACHED HEREON.

标记 MARKS & NOS.	包装及数量 QUANTITY	保险货物项目 DESCRIPTION OF GOODS	保险金额 AMOUNT INSURED
As per Invoice No. SU252022 – J	70 CTNS	CHINESE ROYAL JELLY	JP ¥ 3 385 883. –

总保险金额： JAPANESE YEN THREE MILLION THREE HUNDRED AND EIGHTY TOTAL AMOUNT INSURED: FIVE THOUSAND EIGHT HUNDRED AND EIGHTY THREE ONLY

保费 费率 装载运输工具
PREMIUM AS ARRANGED RATE AS ARRANGED PER CONVERYANCE S. S. BY AIR

开行日期 自 至
SLG. ON OR ABT AS PER AWB from NANJING AIRPORT to NARITA AIRPORT

承保险别 COVERING THE INSTITUTE CARGO CLAUSE (ALL RISKS)
CONDITIONS AND INSTITUTE WAR CLAUSES AND THE INSTITUTE S. . RC. C. CLAUSES I. O. P.

所 保 货 物 ， 如 遇 出 险 ， 本 公 司 凭 本 保 险 单 及 其 他 有 关 证 件 给 付 赔 款 。
CLAIMS, IF ANY, PAYABLE ON SURRENDER OF THIS POLICY TOGETHER WITH OTHER RELEVANT DOCUMENTS.
所 保 货 物 ， 如 发 生 本 保 险 单 项 下 负 责 赔 偿 的 损 失 或 事 故
IN THE EVENT OF ACCIDENT WHEREBY LOSS OR DAMAGE MAY RESULT IN A CLAIM – UNDER THE POLICY IMMEDIATE NOTICE
应 立 即 通 知 本 公 司 下 述 代 理 人 查 勘 。
APPLYING FOR SURVEY MUST BE GIVEN TO THE COMPANY'S AGENT AS MENTIONED HEREUNDER.

赔款偿付地点 AT NARITA (IN JAPAN) 中国人民保险公司江苏省分公司
CLAIM PAYABLE
日期 南京 THE PEOPLE'S INSURANCE CO. OF CHINA
DATE 30 MARCH, 1995 NANJING JIANGSU BRANCH
地址：中国南京市石鼓路 49 号 邮政编码：210005 TEL：（025） 4419969 FAX：（025） 4400253
ADDRESS: 49 SHIGU ROAD. NANJING, CHINA Telex: 34159 ROAD CN

涂 英

DUPLICATE

江 苏 省 土 产 进 出 口 集 团 股 份 有 限 公 司

JIANGSU NATIVE PRODUCE IMPORT & EXPORT (GROUP) CORP.

38 GONG YUAN ROAD, NANJING, CHINA

PACKING LIST

To: Whom it may concern

DATE: MARCH 20 1995

As Per Invoice

No. SU252022 - J

MARKS & NUMBERS

SUMIT IN TRIANGLE

SU252022 - J

NARITA

NO. 1 - 70

DESCRIPTION	PACKAGES	QUANTITY	GROSS	NETS	MEASS
CHINESE ROYAL JELLY DECENOIC ACID 2.161 5% MIN MOISTURE: 66.08% MAX	70 CTNS	700KGS	1050KGS	700KGS	$3.4M^3$

TOTAL: 70 CTNS 700KGS

GRS 1 050 KGS NETS 700.00KGS MEASS $3.400\ M^3$

PRODUCTS BY LAOSHAN FACTORY

PACKING: IN 1KG/PLASTIC BOTTLE 10 KGS/CTN

江苏省土产进出口集团股份有限公司

JIANGSU NATIVE PRODUCE

IMPORT & EXPORT (GROUP) CORP.

范 力

ORIGINAL

1. Goods consigned from (Exporter's business name, address, country) JIANGSU NATIVE PRODUCE I/E (GROUP) CORP.	Reference No. 2048 GENERALIZED SYSTEM OF PREFERENCES **CERTIFICATE OF ORIGIN** (Combined declaration and certificate) **FORM A** Issued in THE PEOPLE'S REPUBLIC OF CHINA (country) See Notes overleaf
2. Goods consigned to (Consignee's name, address, country) SUMITOMO CORPORATION, TOKYO 2 –2 HITOTSUBASHI CHIYODA – KU, TOKYO	
3. Means of transport and route (as far as known) FROM NANJING AIRPORT TO NARITA AIRPORT BY AIR	4. For office use

5. Item number	6. Marks and numbers of packages	7. Number and kind of package, description of goods	8. Origin criterion (see Notes overleaf)	9. Gross weight or other quantity	10. Number and date of invoices
		CHINESE ROYAL JELLY			
SUMIT IN TRIANGEL SU252022 NARITA No. 1 –70		70 CTNS. SAY SEVENTY CTNS		1050 KGS	SU252022 – J 20 MAR, 1995

11. Certification It is hereby certified on the basis of control carried out, that the declaration by the exporters is correct. 余 亚 中华人民共和国 江苏 进出口商品检验局 NANJING, CHINA 24 MAR, 1995	Declaration by the exporter. The undersigned hereby declares that the above and statements are correct: that all the goods were produced in CHINA. And that they comply with the origin requirements specified for those goods in the Generalized System of Preferences for goods exported to (Importing country) JIANGSU NATIVE PRODUCE I & E (GROUP) CORP. NANJING, CHINA MARCH 21, 1995 张敏

ONE COPY

中华人民共和国江苏进出口商品检验局

JIANGSU IMPORT & EXPORT COMMODITY INSPECTION BUREAU

OF THE PEOPLE'S REPUBLIC OF CHINA

副本

COPY

地址：南京市白下路1号

Address：1 Baixia Road
Nanjing

检验证书

日期

电报：南京2914

Cable：2914 NANJING

INSPECTION CERTIFICATE

Date 24 MAR，1995

电话：

Tel：648993

of

QUALITY

发货人：

Consignor JIANGSU NATIVE PRODUCE IMPORT & EXPORT（GROUP）CORP.

受货人：

Consignee

品名：CHINESE ROYAL JELLY
（PRODUCTS BY LAOSHAN FACTORY）

Commodity

标记及号码：

MARK & NO. SUMIT IN TRIANGLE

SU252022－J
NARITA
NO. 1－70

报验数量/重量 70CTNS/700KGS.

Quantity/Weight

Declared

检验结果：

RESULTS OF INSPECTION：

REPRESENTATIVE SAMPLE WAS DRAWN AGAINST THE STANDARD NO. GB9697－88 AND INSPECTED WITH THE RESULTS AS FOLLOWS：

LOT NO.	MOISTURE	DECENOIC ACID
940048	65.7%	2.1765%
940049	66.03%	2.1516%

CONCLUSION：IN CONFORMITY WITH THE CONTRACT NO. 95JN1010J

****

中华人民共和国
江苏
进出口商品检验局

主任检验员

张 荣

ONE COPY

中华人民共和国进出口商品检验局
JIANGSU IMPORT & EXPORT COMMODITY INSPECTION BUREAU
OF THE PEOPLE'S REPUBLIC OF CHINA

副本
COPY

地址：南京市白下路1号
Address：1 Baixia Road
Nanjing

检验证书

日期

INSPECTION CERTIFICATE

Date 24 MAR，1995

电报：南京2914
Cable：2914 NANJING
电话：
Tel：648993

of

QUALITY

发货人：
Consignor JIANGSU NATIVE PRODUCE IMPORT & EXPORT（GROUP）CORP.
受货人：
Consignee ______
品名：CHINESE ROYAL JELLY　　标记及号码：
（PRODUCTS BY LAOSHAN FACTORY）
Commodity ______ MARK & NO. SUMIT IN TRIANGLE

SU252022－J
NARITA
NO. 1－70

报验数量/重量 70CTNS/700KGS.
Quantity/Weight
Declared ______
检验结果：
RESULTS OF INSPECTION：
NO ANTIBIOTIC WAS FOUND THROUGH INSPECTION

CONCLUSION：IN CONFORMITY WITH THE CONTRACT NO. 95JN1010J

中华人民共和国
江苏
进出口商品检验局

主任检验员
张　荣

五、结果分析

1. 单据审核操作流程的准确性与高效性分析。
2. 单据审核处理的合规性分析。

*实验七

国际结算中的贸易融资
（综合实验）

一、实验目的

1. 掌握贸易融资的申请条件。
2. 掌握贸易融资的操作流程。
3. 掌握贸易融资的利息计算。

二、实验原理

（一）出口结算中的贸易融资知识点

出口商在国际贸易中，可以在不同结算方式下，从银行获得各种融资便利。

1. 出口商业发票贴现（Export Invoice Discounting）

出口商业发票贴现指在出口赊销（O/A）方式或承兑交单（D/A）下，出口商以商业发票为抵押到出口地银行申请获得的由银行为其提供贸易融资、应收账款催收、销售分户账管理等服务。出口商业发票贴现业务处理基本程序见图 7－1。

为降低融资风险，出口地银行应审核出口商及进口商资信状况；对提单、发票等商业单据及报关单等进行一致性审核，以确保贸易背景的真实性，同时还应了解出口商品在当前国际市场的行情及变化趋势。

出口商业发票贴现融资中，贴现利息计算公式为：贴现利息＝本金×融资年利率×贴现天数/360。其中，利率以 LIBOR 加点的方式参照各行对贸易融资业务的利率执行。贴现天数一般是办理贴现日到预计收款日的天数上再加上 30 天来计。

出口地银行以进口商到期支付货款为还款来源，如果进口商到期无法支付货款，银行可向出口商行使追索权，收回贴现款项并计收逾期利息。

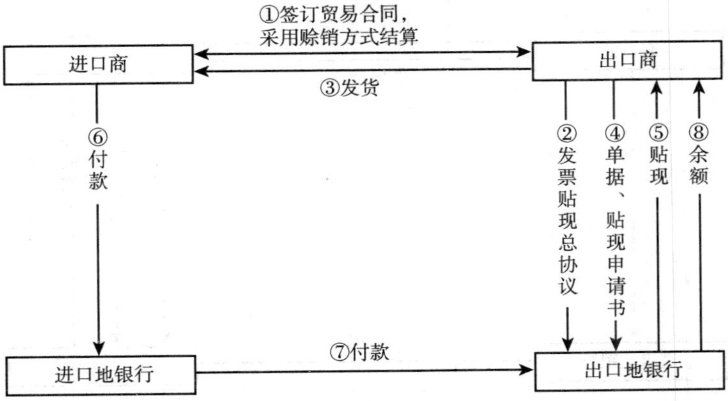

图 7－1　出口商业发票贴现处理基本程序

2. 出口贴现（Export Bill Discount）

出口贴现指在信用证或跟单托收结算方式下，出口商将银行承兑的未到期远期汇票或未到期远期债权卖给银行从而获得的一种短期融资。出口贴现利率按同期外汇流动资金贷款利率计算，期限从贴现日起至预计收汇日止。如果到期远期汇票未获付款人付款，银行拥有对出口商的追索权。信用证下出口贴现业务处理基本程序见图 7－2。

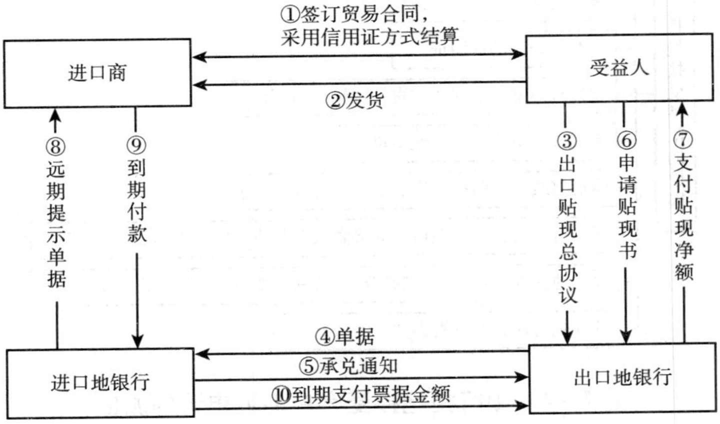

图 7－2　出口贴现处理基本程序

3. 出口押汇（Export Bill Purchase）

出口押汇指在信用证或跟单托收结算方式下，出口商向出口地银行交来单据后凭所交单据为抵押从银行获得的短期资金融通。出口押汇业务处理基本程序见图 7－3。

出口押汇利息计算公式为：押汇利息＝本金×融资年利率×押汇天数/360，出口押汇利率以押汇当日 LIBOR 为基础，考虑银行筹资成本、资信风险等因素后确定。押汇天数从办理押汇日到预计信用证收汇日的天数加上 5～7 天来计。押汇金额比例由银行根据实际情况核定，最高额为单据金额的 100%，银行预扣银行费用、押汇利息后，将净额划入企业账

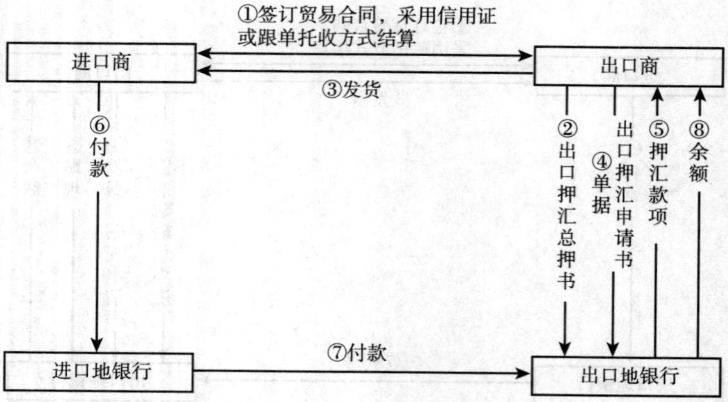

图 7－3　出口押汇处理基本程序

户。如实际收汇日超出押汇的期限，银行将向企业补收押汇利息。为降低风险，银行拒绝接受客户押汇申请的原因见图 7－4。

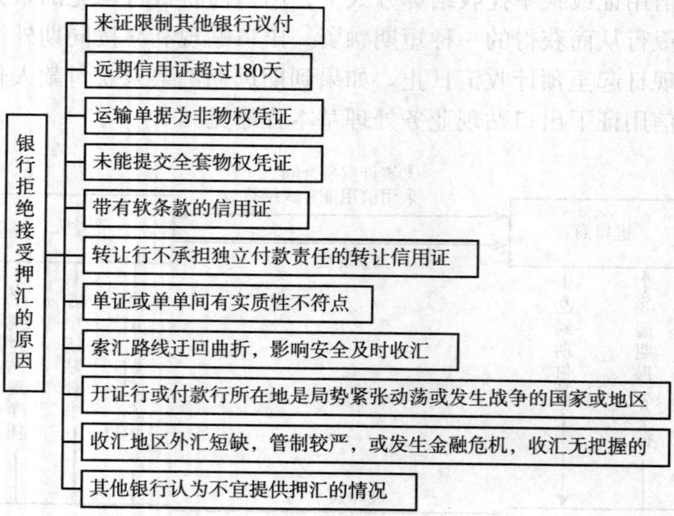

图 7－4　银行拒绝接受客户押汇申请的原因

4. 出口打包放款（Packing Loan）

出口打包放款指在信用证结算方式下，国外进口商不同意预付货款时，出口商可以信用证为抵押向银行申请用于信用证项下货物采购、生产和装运的短期专项贷款。出口打包放款业务处理基本程序见图 7－5。

打包放款融资比例通常不超过 90%，还款的来源在正常情况下为信用证项下的收汇款，在企业不能正常从国外收回货款的情况下，企业必须偿还打包贷款的本金及利息，或允许银行主动从其账户扣划打包贷款的本金及利息。

打包贷款可以使用人民币，也可以使用外汇作为贷款的币种。银行办理打包放款的利息

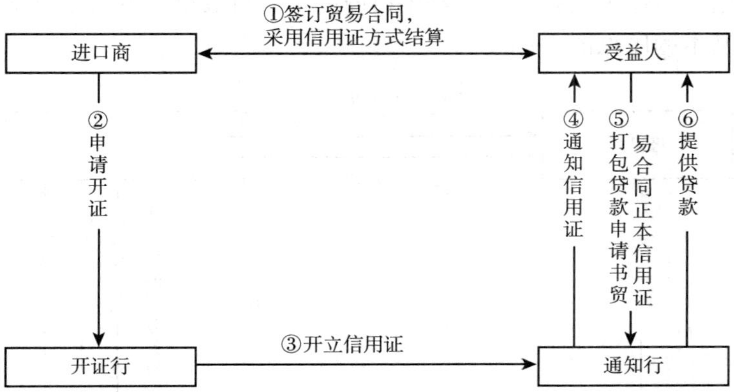

图7－5　出口打包放款处理基本程序

计算公式为：出口打包放款利息＝信用证金额×融资比例（70%～90%）×融资年利率×放款天数/360。放款天数从办理放款日到信用证规定最迟装运日的天数加上30天来计。出口商到银行申请打包放款的条件见图7－6。

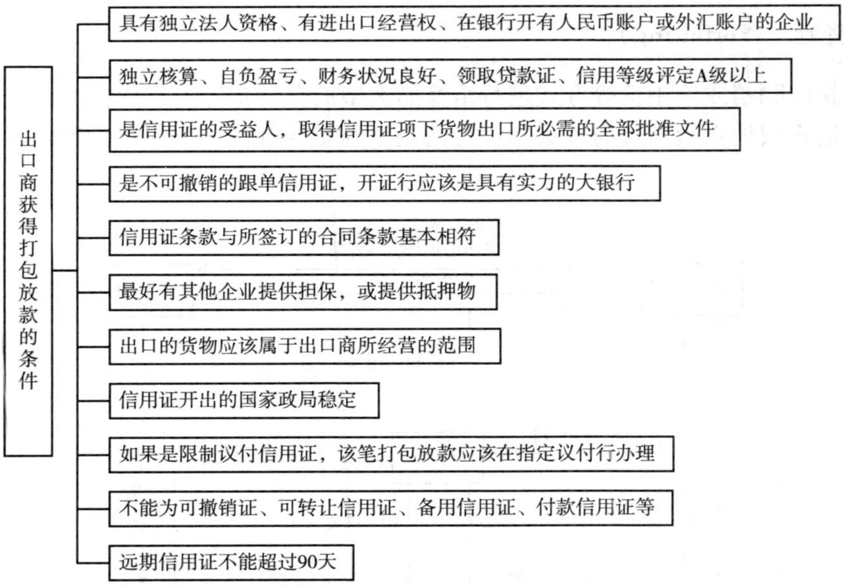

图7－6　出口商获得打包放款的条件

5. 出口保理（Two-Factor Export Factoring）

出口保理业务指在赊销（O/A）、承兑交单（D/A）等非信用证结算方式的出口贸易中，出口商在货物装运后立即将发票、汇票、提单等有关单据卖断给出口保理商（出口地银行），获得银行提供的信用担保、货款催收、销售分类账管理以及贸易融资等金融服务。一般出口保理商提供的融资不超过发票金额的90%，目前国内银行主要做的是出口双保理业务，保理业务中出口保理商是否拥有对出口商的追索权取决于各自银行不同的规定。出口双保理业务处理基本程序见图7-7。

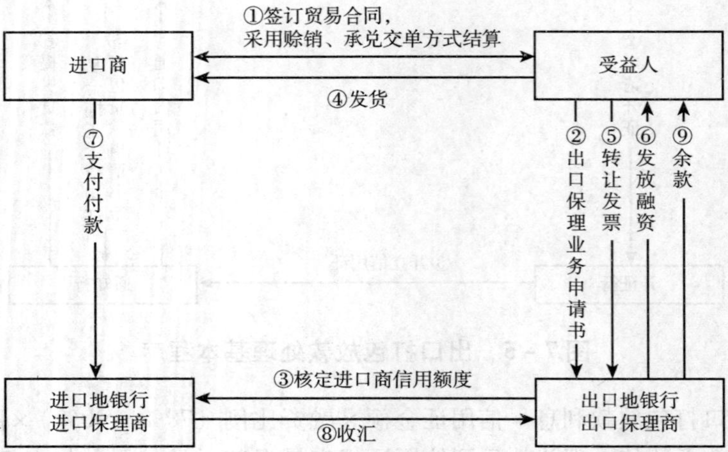

图7-7 出口双保理处理基本程序

6. 福费廷（Forfaiting）

福费廷指以赊销或信用证等方式进行结算的大型成套设备等资本货物出口中，出口商将远期票据无追索权地卖给贴现商或买断银行而获得的短期融资。福费廷业务处理基本程序见图7-8。

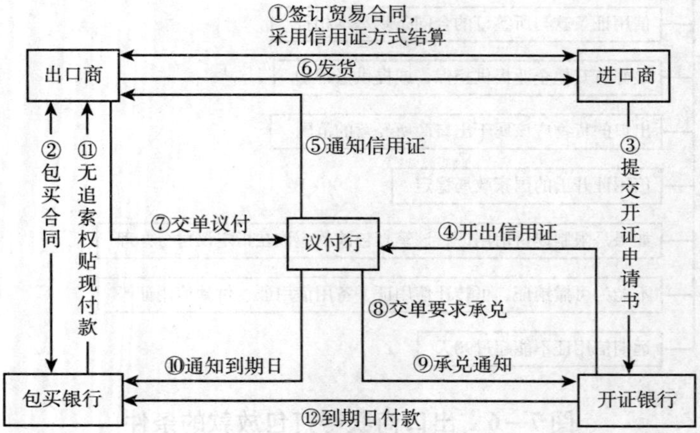

图7-8 福费廷处理基本程序

（二）进口结算中的贸易融资知识点

在进口贸易结算中，银行也可以向进口商提供各种资金便利，为进口商解决资金周转的困难。

1. 进口押汇（Import Bill Advance）

进口押汇指在进口信用证或进口代收结算方式下，进口商可以凭有效凭证和商业单据到进口地银行申请的短期资金融通。进口押汇业务处理基本程序见图7-9。

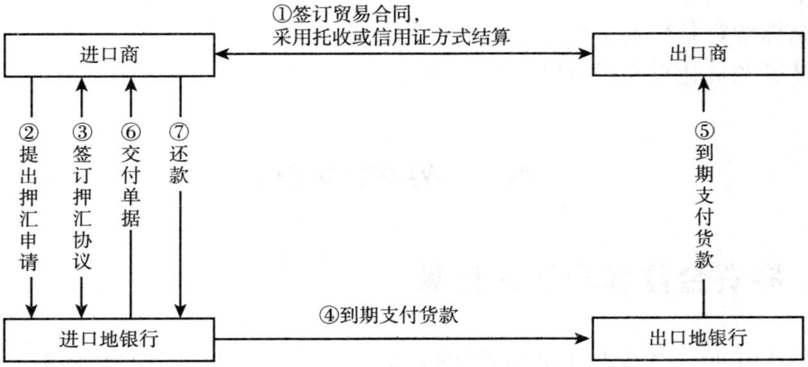

图7-9 进口押汇处理基本程序

进口押汇中押汇利息的计算公式为：押汇利息=本金×融资年利率×押汇天数/360，押汇天数一般与进口货物转卖的期限相匹配，并以销售回笼款项作为押汇的主要还款来源。

2. 提货担保（Shipping Guarantee）

提货担保指在信用证结算方式下，载货船舶早于运输单据到达卸货港时，进口商为了及时提货，避免货物滞港，由进口商或其代理人出具并由银行加签凭以向承运人办理提货手续的一种保函。提货担保业务处理基本程序见图7-10。

实务中，只有运输方式为海运，信用证规定提交全套提单且仅限于信用证项下的进口货物，才能申请提货担保。进口商凭提货担保提取货物后，即使将来收到的单据存在不符点，也不能对银行拒付。

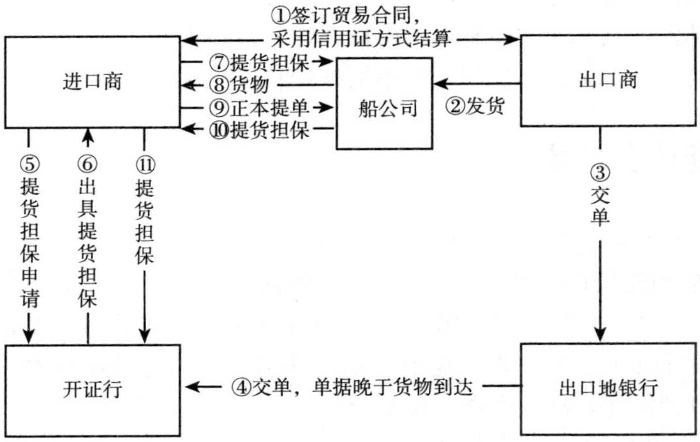

图7-10 提货担保处理基本程序

三、实验内容

1. 国际结算融资业务的操作流程。
2. 国际结算融资条件的审核。
3. 国际结算融资金额和融资利息的计算。

四、实验步骤

（一）融资金额和利息的计算

1. 一笔信用证下，受益人A公司在2008年11月24日到银行申请办理出口押汇。装运日是2008年11月21日，信用证规定的付款条件是提单后30天付款，预计信用证的收汇日为12月21日，押汇利息为4.12%。计算该笔业务中的押汇利息。

2. 一笔信用证下，受益人A公司于2009年11月10日到A银行申请打包贷款。信用证金额为USD500 000.00，信用证开证日期为2009年11月1日，最迟装运日为2009年12月31日。银行审核客户的资信后决定发放80%的款项，按年利率3.43%计息。计算该笔业务实际打包放款金额和打包放款利息。

（二）融资业务的条件

1. 出口商应具备什么条件才能到银行申请办理出口商业发票贴现？
2. 出口商应具备什么条件才能到银行申请办理出口贴现？
3. 出口商应具备什么条件才能到银行申请办理出口押汇？
4. 出口商办理福费廷业务时，应向出口地银行提交哪些材料？
5. 进口商应具备什么条件才能到银行申请办理进口押汇？
6. 进口商应具备什么条件才能到银行申请办理提货担保？

（三）融资业务的操作

1. 出口押汇和出口打包放款在操作上有何差异？

2. 出口商A公司按照巴克莱银行开来的金额为60万英镑，期限为提单后60天的远期信用证出运货物后，将全套单据交给国内A银行要求办理融资业务。A银行将单据寄往花旗银行后，花旗银行向A银行开来承兑电，承诺到期付汇。这笔业务中，出口商A公司可向A银行申请出口押汇还是贴现融资？说明原因。

3. 福费廷业务与出口保理业务操作中有何差异？

4. 福费廷业务与信用证出口押汇操作有何差异？

五、结果分析

1. 国际结算融资品种选择合理性分析。
2. 国际结算融资业务操作合规性分析。

参考文献

1. 陈湛匀．国际结算实务．上海：立信会计出版社，1994
2. 刘晓潮．商业银行信贷及国际结算实验．北京：经济科学出版社，2009
3. 沈家庆．国际结算业务处理．北京：高等教育出版社，2008
4. 苏宗祥，徐捷．国际结算．北京：中国金融出版社，2008
5. 颜世廉，邵新力，丁华南．国际结算．长沙：中南大学出版社，2000
6. 叶玉军，王甘霖．国际贸易结算实务操作与技巧．北京：中国金融出版社，1994
7. 张燕玲．国际结算业务指南．北京：中华工商联合出版社，1995
8. http：//www. boc. cn/
9. http：//intl. 51. net/phparticle/index. php
10. http：//www. 10588. com/html/index. html